FIRESIDE

PARKSIDE

Hooked on Exercise

How to Understand and Manage Exercise Addiction

Rebecca Prussin, M.D.,
Philip Harvey, Ph.D., and
Theresa Foy DiGeronimo

A FIRESIDE / PARKSIDE RECOVERY BOOK
Published by Simon & Schuster
NEW YORK   LONDON   TORONTO   SYDNEY   TOKYO   SINGAPORE

FIRESIDE/PARKSIDE
Simon & Schuster Building
Rockefeller Center
1230 Avenue of the Americas
New York, New York 10020

Library of Congress Cataloging-in-Publication Data

Prussin, Rebecca, 1951–
    Hooked on exercise: how to understand and manage exercise addiction
  Rebecca Prussin, Philip Harvey, and Theresa Foy DiGeronimo.
        p. cm.
    Includes bibliographical references.
        1. Exercise—Psychological aspects.   I. Harvey, Philip D., 1956–.
  II. DiGeronimo, Theresa Foy.   III. Title.
  GV481.2.P78   1992
  613.7'1—dc20   91-27742
                                                                      CIP

ISBN 0-671-76772-0

Designed by Irving Perkins Associates
Manufactured in the United States of America

10 9 8 7 6 5 4 3 2 1

Parkside Medical Services Corporation is a full-service provider of treatment for
alcoholism, other drug addiction, eating disorders, and psychiatric illness.

Parkside Medical Services Corporation
205 West Touhy Avenue
Park Ridge, IL 60058
1-800-PARKSIDE

The self-help programs outlined in this book are presented as a first step toward facing and conquering an exercise addiction. If you try this self-help approach and do not successfully master your need to exercise excessively, we strongly urge you to refer to the Resource Guide in Appendix B, which lists professional intervention programs that can support your efforts to overcome your addiction.

Contents

1

An Addiction Like Other Addictions

Although you may not be aware of it, exercise addiction may be causing you to sacrifice family, career, and/or social opportunities and responsibilities. Renee, twenty-one years old, is about to enter her senior year as an economics major at Columbia University in New York City. When Renee finished her junior year she decided to spend the summer as an intern securities trader at a rather well-known Wall Street firm. At that time, she was finding it very difficult ("Completely impossible!" to use her own words) to balance her new work schedule with her exercise schedule.

Renee had been a track star in high school and continued her cross-country running in college. During her first three college years, Renee spent about three hours *every day* keeping her slender five-foot eight-inch frame in top physical shape. At least one hour of Nautilus workouts and two hours of running became the focus of her daily life. But now, Renee was finding it more and more difficult to squeeze this three hours into her schedule. The commute to Wall Street from her New Jersey home left her no spare morning time; because lunch hours were nonexistent for new traders, the afternoons also gave her no hope of stealing away for a run, and many evenings called for overtime and late train rides home.

Renee was not consoled by the fact that she could fit in her full workout three or four days a week (thanks to some free time on weekends!). Instead she worried that missing *daily* workouts would jeopardize her athletic standing back at college. She also worried because, although the scale said she hadn't gained any weight, she felt fat and unattractive. She also felt let down because the active New York social life she had planned for her summer was being sacrificed to squeeze in time on the exercise bike she bought to compensate for lost running time. Eventually, Renee found that most of her days were spent feeling tense and anxious while worrying that she wouldn't be able to run that night; on the days after a missed workout she felt depressed, guilty, and fatigued.

These negative feelings left Renee feeling bewildered during an apprenticeship period that she had expected would be wonderfully exciting and invigorating. Unfortunately, the withdrawal symptoms caused by exercise addiction overshadowed all of the good and productive things that could have happened. Without clearly understanding why she felt so miserable day after day, Renee decided securities trading was not for her; she quit her job in late July and wrote off the summer as a "disaster."

Renee will now go back to college to resume her school and exercise schedule and all will be back to normal—at least until the next time she is faced with career, family, or social obligations that interfere with her workouts. Renee is addicted to exercise and, as with all addictions, the consequences of the dependency aren't clearly seen until something interferes with the fulfillment of its needs. Renee has already lost valuable work experience and has changed her career goals because she mistook her exercise withdrawal symptoms for job dissatisfaction. Renee is, unfortunately, not an isolated example. Many people have significant problems with exercise addiction.

Are you hooked on exercise? The following quiz will help you determine if you are exercising too much.

		YES	NO
1.	Do you think and talk about exercise more often than you used to?	___	___
2.	Do you daydream about your workouts?	___	___
3.	Do you exercise despite the weather or other negative environmental factors, such as no air conditioning at your gym on the hottest days of the year?	___	___
4.	Do you exercise even when you're sick or injured?	___	___
5.	Do you consistently exercise to improve your mood, to relax, or to combat depression?	___	___
6.	Do you find that you get irritable on days when you can't find the time to exercise?	___	___
7.	Have you ever lied about how often you exercise?	___	___
8.	Do you spend more money than you can realistically afford on exercise-related equipment and/or fees?	___	___
9.	Has anyone ever complained that you exercise too much?	___	___

10. Has your exercise schedule ever interfered with your ability to perform adequately at work?   _____ _____

11. Has exercise ever impaired your relationships?   _____ _____

12. Do you find it difficult to relate to people who are not involved in exercise?   _____ _____

13. Do you find that you enjoy other activities only if you know you'll still have the opportunity to exercise?   _____ _____

14. Do you ever feel terrible, ugly, fat, lazy, worthless, etc., when you don't exercise?   _____ _____

15. Do you feel you must exercise to keep your weight under control or to allow you to eat more?   _____ _____

16. Do you have trouble imagining your life without exercise?   _____ _____

If you answered yes to eight or more of these questions, it's possible you are addicted to exercise.

The word *addiction* is not a trendy label tagged on to the word *exercise* to grab your attention and then to be acknowledged later as literary license rather than truth. In the strict sense of its clinical definition, people hooked on exercise are indeed "addicts." They are people who abuse exercise in the same way other addicts abuse alcohol, drugs, cigarettes, gambling, or shopping. They react to the same kind of psychological stimuli—they experience the same characteristics of tolerance, craving, dependence, withdrawal, and denial, and they, too, suffer the negative physical, psychological, and social consequences of their addictive behavior.

Exercise means different things to different people. To avoid any misunderstanding, we define exercise as repetitive muscular movement that is intentionally used to obtain specific benefits such as muscular strength, weight loss, cardiac fitness, increased skill proficiency, or simply enjoyment. Based on this definition, the repetitive shoveling movement that builds muscular strength in a construction worker is not exercise as we define it. This isn't to say that there are no benefits derived from this activity but rather that we are limiting our scope to exercise activities that are engaged in as a form of recreation. Thus, walking or biking as a means of transportation is not the same as walking or biking for exercise.

Daily exercise, in contrast to many other potentially addictive behaviors, can be strictly beneficial with no adverse consequences. It is only when a regular exercise pattern is accompanied by signs of dependence—when it starts to run your life—that it becomes problematic. Dependence on an activity or substance, be it alcohol or exercise, occurs concurrently with other emotional troubles and serves two important functions for the user: the activity helps to produce a feeling of calm and it provides an alternative focus of interest. In this way, addictions serve as psychological defenses.

Addiction is not easily defined because variables such as the substance or activity, genetic makeup, and individual personality affect the phenomenon. For the purposes of this book, we define addiction as any repetitive behavior that (1) is marked by eventual tolerance which, at the same dosage, is associated with decreased desirable affects; (2) is craved because it is needed to maintain an optimal level of physical and psychological functioning; (3) results in a dependence that impairs a person's capacity to cope with other people, activities, and/or emotional demands; and (4) is marked by denial, which serves to obscure the consequences of the behavior. When a person's use of exercise meets these four criteria, it can be said that that person is addicted to exercise.

BASIC CHARACTERISTICS

Although each person's addiction is unique, all addictions have fundamental similarities. As you read through the following sections you'll see how these characteristics apply to addictions in general and then how an exercise addict may experience them.

TOLERANCE

Addictive substances and activities initially offer positive reinforcement that encourages an individual to continue in their use. Alcohol, for example, can be pleasing to the taste and can complement the enjoyment of many foods. It also may give casual drinkers a release from tension and a sense of calm. It can lower inhibitions and allow people to be more social or more assertive than they would normally be. In the same way, some drugs offer a temporary feeling of euphoria; gambling gives feedback in the thrill of a possible win, and exercise gives increased feelings of emotional and physical well-being and improved self-esteem.

As an individual continues to use the substance or activity on a regular schedule and is continually exposed to its effects, a tolerance for the initial reaction can develop. Once this happens, the initial benefits will no longer be attainable at the same dosage or level of activity. It will take more alcohol or drugs to reach the same level of relaxation or euphoria, and it will take more winning experiences or higher stakes for the gambler and more physical activity for the exerciser to feel the same thrill in performance. Tolerance is reached when repeated use causes a decrease in the intensity of the reaction.

When Joe, for example, began playing squash, forty-five minutes of court time was plenty to give him full enjoyment of the game and a good physical workout. During each match, he felt he had reached his target rate of cardiovascular and aerobic functioning; he often felt slightly out of breath, and his stamina was pushed to an enjoyable limit.

Joe has played forty-five-minute matches three times a week for six months, but he no longer enjoys the same level of physical pleasure. "I feel like I've just warmed up when it's time to go," he says. "I don't feel like I've really exercised when I finish without being out of breath or without feeling my heart pounding." Starting next week Joe has scheduled the court for back-to-back sessions so he can get in at least an hour and a half of playtime. Joe is showing signs of physical and psychological tolerance for this activity. This doesn't mean he's addicted; it just means his body is adjusting to repeated doses of the workout. However, as explained below, if he also begins to show signs of craving or dependence, his high tolerance level will make it more and more difficult for him to fulfill his need.

CRAVING

As the body builds up a tolerance, an individual may crave the feelings that accompanied the initial doses of the addictive substance or activity. Characterized by an intense and sometimes uncontrollable desire to repeat the experience, cravings can cause individuals to reorder their priorities and to ignore other important obligations and activities in order to fulfill the need.

When craving begins, the person may begin to lie and attempt to deceive others to obtain the desired substance or activity. A person who craves alcohol or drugs may, for example, keep a small amount in a desk drawer at work or even sneak off for a quick dose to relieve a craving. A gambler, exerciser, or shopper may suddenly leave work for a short period to fulfill the need for a "fix."

Also, the craving may be satisfied in ways or at times that do not offer the individual any semblance of pleasure. Drinkers or drug users, for example, may fulfill a craving knowing in advance that they'll feel guilty and shameful when it causes them to miss an important family function. Cyclists, joggers, and walkers may crave a workout when it's cold and raining or while suffering from an injury. If the craving is strong enough, they will complete their exercise routine despite the discomfort or pain. At this point, family and friends may recognize the symptoms of craving and see that a problem is in the making.

Consider Frank, who has been playing golf for twenty years. Frank had always found golf to be a relaxing way to unwind from the pressures of his job as an advertising account executive. But lately, Frank has been playing at unusual and inopportune times. Last week he rushed his wife and kids home from a family barbecue so he could get in a few holes before dark. Due to his wife's reluctance to leave at once, it was almost dark when they arrived home. Slamming the door behind him, Frank stormed out of the house with his clubs flung over his back to go to a driving range instead of the golf course. Nothing was going to keep him from satisfying his need to play. Today, Frank canceled an important business meeting because he had an "urge" to play.

Frank's cravings have just begun to affect his ability to meet social and business obligations, and his family and coworkers have only a vague sense that something is wrong. If Frank continues to make golf his highest priority, he may soon find himself hooked and dependent on routine and increasing doses of golf to maintain his normal easygoing demeanor.

Dependence and Withdrawal

Dependency exists when a dose of a substance or activity is required in order for a person to function at the same level of performance he or she was accustomed to before beginning the addictive behavior. One can certainly drink, gamble, smoke cigarettes, shop, exercise, or even inject heroin on an occasional or intermittent basis without being dependent on that behavior. Many activities that *could* cause dependence are relatively benign at infrequent intervals or lower doses; addiction relies on repeated use on a routine basis. Dependence most often develops slowly and follows behind the use, tolerance, and craving sequence characteristic of addiction development.

Dependence is insidious in that, as long as the substance or activity is used in regular doses, it's difficult to detect by either the addict or an observer. The presence of dependency can be determined only when the behavior is abruptly withheld and withdrawal symptoms occur.

Once dependence has developed, a need can become so intense that physical or emotional disturbances will result if the substance or activity is stopped. Substances like alcohol, drugs, cigarettes, or caffeine that are taken directly into the body can cause physical withdrawal symptoms such as sweating, chills, trembling, increased heart rate, and high blood pressure; with alcohol and certain drugs, withdrawal can cause seizures and even death. Addictive activities such as gambling, shopping, and exercising have the potential to result in a psychological dependency that can grow into an emotional and uncontrollable craving for the activity. When deprived of it, individuals experience psychological withdrawal through feelings of deprivation and uneasiness that can manifest themselves in irritability, anxiety, guilt, or depression. This probably happens because the activity is not available to act as a defense against the basic problem(s). It is especially interesting that emotional withdrawal symptoms can be brought on by the mere anticipation of deprivation. If a gambler, shopper, or exerciser *thinks* that there won't be time for his or her addictive behavior, it's enough to activate symptoms of withdrawal.

Dependence and withdrawal are closely linked characteristics of an exercise addiction. Once an exerciser has followed the addictive progression through use, tolerance, craving, and dependence, an interruption of the exercise activity often brings on withdrawal symptoms. These symptoms may show themselves in physical difficulties such as lethargy or muscle stiffness and in emotional problems such as anxiety, self-deprecation, ill-temper, or depression. The fear of reexperiencing these symptoms can cause an addicted person to become increasingly dependent on the addictive behavior as he or she attempts to prevent the recurrence of withdrawal. It is at this stage of an addiction that the behavior may be practiced routinely despite the fact that it brings less or even no pleasure; now it simply functions to help avoid the discomforts of withdrawal. In effect, a formerly pleasurable activity now becomes an *avoidance response*—a behavior performed only to *avoid* the possibility of feeling worse than before the activity was ever initiated.

Susan is a thirty-two-year-old real-estate broker who likes to jog five to seven miles a day six or seven days a week. Her job affords her a flexible schedule that has made it easy to accomplish this goal for the last two years. Once, last January, however, Susan was not able to maintain this routine and learned for the first time that she might have a problem with exercise. Susan attended a three-day brokers' conference in Boston, which she planned to extend into a six-day vacation. Due to her schedule, two feet of snow, and the unavailability of an indoor running track, Susan was not able to run at all. At first, this was merely annoying to Susan as she participated in her convention duties and festivities. However, by the second day of the conference she found herself in a very unpleasant mood. She was angry at the weather, at the fact that the recreational accommodations did not include a running track, and at herself for not coming prepared to run in the snow. By the end of the three-day conference, Susan was uncharacteristically irritable, tired, and filled with guilt pangs for being (as she described herself), "lazy, self-indulgent, and gluttonous." By twelve noon when the conference ended, Susan was on her way back home. She canceled her vacation plans because she could not wait another day to go running. "In fact," she thought, "I'll run ten miles tonight to make up for some of my lost time."

During her run that evening, Susan felt almost euphoric. She realized how much she needed her exercise routine, and although she was running just as well as before she missed the three convention days, she vowed never to skip any more days for any reason. After her run, Susan felt calm and content.

As long as she is able to squeeze in her running time each day, Susan will not have to experience withdrawal; no one will know her moods are dependent on exercise, and she will be able to maintain her usual proficiency at work. However, as her tolerance and craving levels climb (as they typically do) her ability to meet her needs will probably lessen and her withdrawal symptoms will potentially escalate to include depression, anxiety, and the accompanying self-deprecating thoughts, as well as the physical sensations of bloatedness, sluggishness, and lethargy that she experienced in Boston. Like all addicts, in order to remain in control of her exercise and avoid withdrawal at any cost she will forfeit many things that could be important or pleasurable such as business trips or vacations where it might be difficult to exercise. For Susan, nothing could possibly be more important than her need to run, so any activity that impinged on the fulfillment of that need would be associated with the negative symptoms of withdrawal.

Traditionally, addicts are trapped in a vicious cycle that begins with an ostensibly innocuous venture into a behavior that may once have seemed exceptionally positive. Deprived of this behavior, they experience depression, anxiety, and low levels of self-esteem, which they futilely attempt to manage by using ever-increasing doses of the substance or activity. They must continue on the cycle despite its now unpleasant aspects or risk crashing back into the physical and psychological pains of deprivation.

DENIAL

Like all addicts, exercise addicts will tend to deny a problem until the cycle has picked up momentum and developed the potential to cause substantial personal, professional, and/or financial chaos. Denial is a defense mechanism that occurs in many different psychological conditions, but because it is so common in addictions, it is viewed as one of the primary characteristics. Denial is the refusal to recognize the problems, and then rationalizing to explain the consequences.

Alcohol and exercise addicts use denial to
1. modify perspectives
   alcohol addict: "I haven't been drinking."
   exercise addict: "I do not exercise too much. I know people who exercise far more than I do."
2. modify motives
   alcohol addict: "I was drinking because I was angry."
   exercise addict: "I need to exercise every day in order to maintain my weight."
3. modify amount
   alcohol addict: "I only had two drinks."
   exercise addict: "I had no idea I was at the gym for so long."
4. modify consequences
   alcohol addict: "We got divorced, but it had nothing to do with drinking."
   exercise addict: "My knees would be in bad shape even if I weren't running."

Denial alters the way we think about the world. As you can see by the sample statements above, denial makes it very easy to come up with excuses or to avoid reality in other ways. If you want to adequately self-diagnose, you'll have to try to get around the denial process. One way to do this is to take a devil's-advocate position with yourself and try to see your behavior from alternative perspectives. You might, for example, switch roles and try to imagine why someone you are having a relationship with might get upset when all weekend evening plans have to be cut short so you'll be able to get enough sleep before your 5:30 A.M. run. Or you might imagine you are a medical doctor listening to your own list of physical complaints; then give back to yourself the kind of rational response you would expect from an objective, yet knowledgeable, person. If you are addicted to exercise, you'll find, after this kind of self-evaluation, that denial has been enabling you to maintain your addiction because it obscures the negative aspects and because you yourself have willingly believed the denial statements.

This denial, coupled with the dynamics of tolerance, craving, dependence, and withdrawal, makes excessive exercising an addiction like other addictions. And like other addictions it takes time and patience to recognize the problem and then determine a nonthreatening way to deal with it.

ADDICTION SWITCHING

Regular exercise can be used as a positive alternative to many other addictive behaviors because it is incompatible with negative activities such as overeating, smoking, and drinking. In fact, officials of the New York Road Runners Club (one of the major running organizations in the United States) have told us that some of their most determined runners are recovering alcoholics. This is not surprising; exercise is very often a component of addiction treatment programs because it can aid in the process of recovering from negative activities and it provides an excellent way to recover self-esteem and to develop a sense of mastery over one's self and one's environment.

Because exercise shares characteristics with other addictions, there is one situation where it can be a negative alternative—that is when an addiction has a specific under-lying cause that is ignored. In that case the person may simply decide to exercise for all of the same reasons that he or she used to drink, smoke, gamble, or binge-eat. Unfor-tunately, because exercise has the potential to become addic-tive in its own right, a straight switch from one "negative" activity to exercise can leave the underlying problem un-touched and still potentially life destructive.

People, for example, who treat major depression with food eat constantly to make themselves feel better, despite the fact that food is not a cure for depression. If they de-cide that they are tired of being overweight, they might switch their attention from food to exercise with the same excessive involvement and with the same need to escape their unhappy feelings. Now, hooked on exercise in place of food, the underlying problem of depression is still not being addressed.

Healthy exercise *is* an excellent way to counter addictions. But it should never be used merely to replace one excessive or abusive activity with another; if it is, you'll probably get hooked. Here are some hints to help you make sure that your exercise program is not merely a form of addiction switching.

1. Make sure when you're breaking an addiction that exercise is not your only life-style change. You cannot sim-ply replace a negative behavior with another kind of behav-ior. You need to broaden your participation in other activities and change your circle of contacts. Your former addiction was negative because it had the potential to harm you physi-cally or psychologically and because it was all-consuming. Don't let exercise assume these characteristics.

2. Keep exercise in proper perspective. Even professional

athletes try to maintain multiple types of training and keep workouts under control. Exercise is supposed to be fun; if it becomes a dreary obligation, you are probably doing it to satisfy an unhealthy need.

3. Try to understand the factors that led to your previous addiction. If those underlying causes are not addressed, anything you substitute has the potential to become addictive. The following chapters will help you identify possible roots of previous and exercise addictions.

2

Exercise as an Avoidance Behavior

My workouts take up so much time I just don't have time for anything else.

In most cases, exercise addiction is time consuming. It takes twenty-five-year-old Jack almost three hours to complete his training routine of running ten miles, completing a one-hour Nautilus workout, and doing a couple of fifteen-minute stints on the stair machine. His rationale is that this daily workout keeps him in shape for his weekend races. Add to this exercise routine time the time it takes to shower, get to and from the gym, stretch his muscles afterward, and treat his sore feet and it's no wonder Jack has little time for dating.

Forty-year-old Meg, too, feels the time pinch when she exercises. As an investment banker, she very often has piles of at-home paperwork to sift through. But more often than not, she carries it back to the office untouched because her after-work aerobic and weight workouts leave her tired and with too little time to do a thorough job.

Jack and Meg both balk at the thought of cutting down on their exercise time, even though this would obviously free up more time for him to establish relationships or for her to reduce her growing paper load and relieve the pressure of always being behind. "My workout time is the best part of my day," says Jack. "It makes me feel involved and active and productive. I meet lots of people at the gym, so it's not like I don't socialize; I just don't have time for formal dating." Meg concurs. "My business is so hectic, I need time to unwind. An intense workout gives me a carefree feeling afterward that counters the pressure inherent in my type of work." Jack and Meg believe what they say, but in truth, it's not just a love of exercise that keeps them so busy; it's also the drive to avoid uncomfortable life situations that has pushed them into obsessive exercise regimes.

Are you using exercise as an avoidance tactic? Answer yes or no to the following questions to find out.

	YES	NO
1. Do you find that there are times when exercise makes it difficult to keep up with social or work demands?	____	____
2. Are there things that you used to do regularly, occupationally, or socially that have been replaced by exercise?	____	____
3. Does exercise regularly provide a way to "not think" or to "get away"?	____	____
4. Do you find that your exercise frequency and intensity tracks the level of outside stresses in your life?	____	____
5. Would you become defensive if someone accused you of "hiding" behind exercise?	____	____

Two or more yes responses indicate that excessive exercise may be a symptom of a need to avoid other problems in your life.

Avoidance behaviors are common, but ineffective, methods of problem management. Although using alcohol or drugs is a more commonly recognized and clearly destructive avoidance tactic, excessive exercise is an equally negative way to deal with problems. These behaviors are rooted in fears that are based on an *actual* or *anticipated* failure in an important activity. Life is full of experiences we all would like to avoid if we could; some people avoid establishing or maintaining personal relationships, intimacy, and social contacts, while others try to dodge marital, parental, financial, or career responsibilities. After a period of encounters with disagreeable experiences, it's completely natural to look for some way to stop the unpleasantness.

It is widely believed that the ability to control adverse situations through avoidance behaviors is the product of what's called the two-factor learning theory. The theory proposes that if two things consistently happen together, a person will soon learn to associate the two. Because Jack's dating experiences, for example, have been a series of disappointing disasters (at least from his perspective), he has learned to associate dating or even the thought of dating with a host of negative feelings. And because Meg has consistently found herself feeling resentful, angry, underappreciated, and overworked each time she does her paperwork at home, she now automatically associates working at home with these negative emotions.

Once the association is made, the second factor kicks in. The second aspect of the theory says that the likelihood of repeating a certain behavior depends on how much we like the feedback we get from it. Jack has learned that a highly structured and time-consuming exercise routine relieves him of dating worries and insecurities. So too, Meg has found that she can completely avoid the negative emotional consequences of working at home by delegating her "free" time to exercise. For both Jack and Meg, the positive feedback of their avoidance behaviors encourages them to repeat the action. Neither recognizes, however, the association of exercise with the avoidance of feelings because both have plausible reasons to support that particular workout pattern.

The mere anticipation of an unpleasant situation is often enough to promote an avoidance reaction. As Meg unloads her briefcase onto her desk at home, the act alone cues her to go out and exercise. In the same way, if someone at work suggests to Jack that they double date or (even more threatening) set up a blind date, Jack, in anticipation of a painful experience, will feel the need to stick to his scheduled workout and use it as an excuse. Similarly, people who are experiencing marital difficulties may decide that it's time to go for a run as soon as they hear their spouse enter the house. Having been conditioned in the past to believe that one event will inevitably lead to personal discomfort, they may continually use exercise as a proven remedy to head off unpleasantness before it has a chance to start. The more often the use of exercise successfully interrupts and delays negative experiences, the more likely it is that people will be encouraged to continue using it as an avoidance strategy and thus develop an addiction.

THE ADDICTION

Unlike obsessive-compulsives, who must structure exercise in advance to maintain a rigidly planned schedule, avoidance exercisers often spontaneously use workouts whenever the possibility of trouble arises, because exercise offers them an ideal way to avoid personal problems. As soon as a young woman asks Jack to have lunch with her, for instance, he can feel justified in refusing her invitation by reminding himself that he needs to make up for his rain-postponed run last night. So he heads for the nearest gym. Meg, too, feels the need for an aerobic workout at the very moment her boss decides she should spend the evening reviewing a client's portfolio. After a time, fewer women seem to ask Jack out and Meg discovers that her boss has limited patience when reports are consistently late.

As noted earlier, alcohol and drug addictions are sometimes more readily noticed and addressed than avoidance-based exercise addictions. If, for example, Jack or Meg chose to avoid their problems by drinking their "free" time away, they would eventually suspect, along with their friends and colleagues, that the behavior was unusual and wonder if there was an underlying unresolved problem. The consequences of compounding an original problem with the added problems of addiction would also become more notably apparent. That's why avoidance-based *exercise* addiction is in some ways more insidious than others with clear danger signals. Because exercise is a socially acceptable way to spend time, and because exercise is viewed as a self-improvement tool, the addicts and their family and friends often are not aware that the focus on fitness is potentially self-destructive.

There are two obvious indicators of avoidance-based exercise addiction. Avoidance behavior is the most likely factor in exercise addiction if exercise doesn't reduce outside pressures in the long run but consistently multiplies them. It is also likely that a person is abusing exercise if he or she exercises more when there is more to avoid (which consequently increases life stress) and exercises less in periods of relative calm. This happens because in avoidance situations exercise addiction generally intensifies in equal proportion to the intensity of the ongoing problem. The more frequently people who use avoidance tactics find themselves in situations that they want to avoid, the more often they'll use exercise as a problem-solving method.

THE PROBLEM

Because we all look for ways to avoid consistently negative situations and feelings, avoidance behaviors appear to be instinctive, self-protective reactions. Avoidance certainly is often a viable temporary solution because it enables us to put some distance between ourselves and our anxieties. In a positive application of avoidance, staying away from a tense situation for a while can buy some time to calm down and decide how to face the difficulty and deal with it.

The problem with avoidance behaviors, however, is that they may be used continually as an easy way out that will never offer an appropriate solution for an ongoing problem. If Jack uses his exercise regimen to avoid all offers of dates and to rationalize his lack of time to date, he'll never address the real reason he feels uncomfortable with women and will therefore deprive himself of the opportunity to develop an intimate relationship. Meg's avoidance of her negative feelings about at-home work keeps her from confronting the reasons why she feels angry about having such a heavy workload. Meg gets upset because she believes it is not humanly possible to accomplish the amount of work dumped on her each day; so perhaps she needs to be more assertive and explain her concerns to her boss. But as long as exercise keeps the negative feelings at bay, she will neither face the problem nor speak to her boss, and so it will continue. We use these same avoidance tactics in a variety of nonexercise situations. If, for example, one leaves the room every time his or her spouse wants to talk about the tension in their marriage, the problem cannot be resolved.

Avoidance behaviors are often inappropriate solutions because they have the potential to compound the original problem. In a vicious cycle, what we avoid today is likely to increase in intensity tomorrow. Then as the pressure increases, we tend to avoid with more frequency and so the pressure increases even more. The longer Jack takes himself out of the dating scene, the more difficult it becomes for him to meet desirable women. The more often he successfully avoids dating, the more he'll be convinced that he's an undesirable mate and therefore shouldn't even try. In Meg's case, exercise enables her to temporarily ignore her feelings that her boss is taking advantage of her. But avoiding the problem and the work only causes the paperwork and her resentment to multiply.

Although exercise can mask the discomfort we feel, at the same time it makes the problems worse. When life's problems get tougher to bear, they need more, not less, of our attention if we expect to control and remedy them. Excessive exercise routines keep some people from giving their problems the focused attention they need.

You may find it easier to grasp the destructive nature of avoidance-based exercise addiction by visualizing how the same process affects alcoholics. If people drink every time they have a lot of work to do, they'll never quit drinking if they always have work to do. Since they can't get work done because they're drinking, there is always a reason to drink and so the addiction and the work problems intensify concurrently. This too is true with exercise addiction.

THE REMEDY

It is well known that exercise has the ability to reduce depression and anxiety. If, for example, the boss criticizes you or if your spouse disappoints you, a long walk, a vigorous workout, or a twenty-minute round with a punching bag will make you feel better and think more objectively. But if you find that you continually use exercise to respond to every stressful situation and have answered yes to the majority of questions in the quiz above, you've created a situation that may interfere with your ability to handle life's problems constructively. The following Three-Step Remedy will help you stop avoiding and start facing the problems that could be keeping you from enjoying a peaceful and productive life. In Step One you'll identify your stress triggers. In Step Two you'll build coping skills, and in Step Three, you'll learn some stress-management techniques that can be used to cope with stress rather than avoid it.

STEP ONE: IDENTIFY YOUR STRESS TRIGGERS

We all have stress triggers. These are the activities, situations, or responsibilities that set off our stress responses. For some, it is public speaking that makes their heart pound, for others traffic jams bring on headaches, for new parents the sound of never-ending crying can be nerve-racking. For Meg it was at-home paperwork that caused feelings of anxiety and anger; whereas for Jack it was dating that made him anxious and depressed. The relationship between stress and exercise addiction is found in the presence of frequent and intense stress combined with lack of flexibility in the reaction. So, as the activities that serve as stress triggers increase in frequency, the need for exercise increases.

You may be able to identify your stress trigger quite readily because for some people the connection is obvious. It's not unusual to hear exercise addicts zero in immediately on the source of their addiction with comments like: "When my husband comes home from work, I go out to the gym. That way I don't have to hear him complain about the messy house or awful meals. By the time I return, he's engrossed in a TV show and leaves me alone." Or, "The more the telephone rings at work, the more I think about getting to the gym for my lunchtime workout."

If you've answered yes to the majority of questions in the quiz earlier in this chapter but aren't sure exactly what it is that you're avoiding, you need to do some detective work to analyze the role exercise is playing in your life. The Stress Degree (SD) Ladder and Scale below will help you pinpoint and measure your daily stresses. Zero (0) represents complete relaxation and 100 represents complete panic—the worst possible state of terror that you can imagine. All the points in between represent different degrees of amounts of stress. When you feel more than 50 SDs, you are experiencing the effects of a significant stress trigger. A score of 50 might be recorded when you're interrupted for the tenth time and you slam your fist on the desk and yell at the unsuspecting intruder, "What do you want?!" Or when your children have spent twenty minutes whining and you finally stomp your foot and insist, "That's enough!" You might even reach 50 when you're filling out tax forms and finally throw your pen on the floor when you're once again referred back to another incoherent instruction form. Measuring SDs will help you find your stress triggers, and then you can learn to eliminate or manage them. Once the stress trigger is identified and under control, you'll find that your need for obsessive exercise will also come under your control.

Meg focused on her stress level one day and marked the

chart accordingly. Following Meg's Stress Degree Scale on page 35 we can see that the mornings are relatively stress free. She finds her 7:00 A.M. commute to work slightly stressful; an 11:00 disagreement with a coworker annoying. But neither sends her SDs over 50. As the work begins to pile up around 3:00 her level of stress also builds. One-half hour before quitting time at 5:00, Meg realizes that once again no matter how quickly she works, she'll have to take home paperwork. With that realization her SDs soar. Once home, Meg has a stressful dinner and then faces the brimming briefcase at 7:00; SDs soar again and it's off to the gym. Meg tracked her SDs the following day as well. She found that on that day the workload was lighter because her boss was out of town, the stress degrees lower, and without yet making a conscious connection between the two she decided to skip her night of aerobics and relax by watching a favorite movie on TV.

Now you try it on the charts on page 36. Remember that stress triggers fluctuate in intensity from one day to the next, but if you're using exercise as an avoidance tactic you'll find that the days you have the strongest cravings for exercise will be on the days when your stress degrees rise over 50. Use this chart for several days during especially active exercise times, and your trigger may soon become evident.

STEP TWO: GRADUALLY BUILD COPING SKILLS

Once you've identified the problem that you're avoiding through excessive exercise routines, you can begin to learn how to deal with it. This would be easy to do if it were a simple matter of recognizing the problem and then saying, "Oh, now that I see what I'm avoiding I just won't do it anymore." But usually it's not that easy. When Meg recognizes the connection between paperwork and exercise, for

STRESS DEGREES

Record Tension Level Hourly or When It Elevates or Decreases Suddenly

Highest	Morning	Afternoon	Evening	Early Morning
100				
90			X	
80				
70		X		
60				
50		X		
40				
30	X X			
20				
10				
0				
Lowest	7 8 9 10 11 12	1 2 3 4 5 6	7 8 9 10 11 12	1 2 3 4 5 6

Record Below Any Experience of Tension Above 50 SDs

	Antecedent (what happened just before)	Behavior (your experience of tension)	Consequence (what happened afterward)
1	My "to do" work pile began to build	My heart pounds I clench my jaw	I became angry & shoved the work into my case & stormed out the door
2	I tried to convince myself to begin doing the work I brought home	I slammed a few doors & swore under my breath	I went out to my aerobics class
3			
4			

STRESS DEGREES

Record Tension Level Hourly or When It Elevates or Decreases Suddenly

Highest	Morning	Afternoon	Evening	Early Morning
100 90				
80 70				
60 50				
40 30				
20 10				
0 Lowest	7 8 9 10 11 12	1 2 3 4 5 6	7 8 9 10 11 12	1 2 3 4 5 6

Record Below Any Experience of Tension Above 50 SDs

	Antecedent (what happened just before)	Behavior (your experience of tension)	Consequence (what happened afterward)
1			
2			
3			
4			

example, she might want to face the situation, be disciplined, and refuse to work out until every last bit of work is completed. However, we all know that that won't be easy or even sensible for her to work out until every last bit of work is completed. However, do. First of all, Meg is addicted to exercise, and, as with any addiction, abrupt withdrawal is not the easy or desirable way to end it. Also, the negative feelings that Meg has about working at home won't disappear just because she decides to tough it out; they'll probably multiply without her outlet. The goal in this Step Two is to plan small, gradual changes in the way you deal with your stress trigger that will help you eventually reduce reliance on the exercise habit and will at the same time help you change and/or better manage your response to stress.

We cannot fully discuss how to gradually cope with all the possible stress triggers that lead people to use exercise as an avoidance tactic. Your job is to identify your problem area and then make a deal with yourself that you will attempt to face the situation one small step at a time. Meg became motivated to change her avoidance tactics when she recognized that much of her exercise wasn't really fun or invigorating but was still necessary to keep her from feeling anxious. After Meg realized that her workouts had become no more than coping strategies, she no longer wished to remain dependent upon them. To illustrate the process, let's follow Meg through her addiction-breaking strategy:

Meg's first step is to overcome her anxiety about bringing work home. The very thought of the extreme difficulty of doing her job as thoroughly as she would like activates her stress responses. So Meg decided that she would load up her briefcase but then promised herself that she had to do only thirty minutes of work at home. That doesn't sound like much, but it's a long time when you're doing something you don't want to do. In this way, Meg could slowly get over her fear of opening the briefcase and being saddled with several hours of work and she knew that after the thirty minutes, she would still have time to exercise.

After one week of this schedule, Meg realized that she could get a lot done in those thirty minutes and she felt a bit more prepared to face each new day at work. Now she was ready to increase the time to forty-five minutes (but not one minute more), and although she was losing some time from her workout, she wasn't giving it up completely.

During the second week, Meg found that she didn't need to work for forty-five minutes—most often half an hour was all she needed to catch up enough on the day's work so that she would stop falling behind. It had always seemed like so much that she had imagined the at-home work would impose on *all* her free time. Now she had her work done *and* free time. On the nights when she had more than thirty minutes of work, Meg kept her promise to herself if she felt any anxiety and stopped when time was up. Occasionally, however, Meg would work through an entire evening without any sense of stress or tension. She had shattered her mental connection between the *expectation* of too much work and her *feelings* of anxiety. It became clear that it was the *idea* of work that Meg was avoiding, not the work itself.

As is typical of avoidance-based exercise addicts, the need to exercise serves to meet the need to avoid a problem. As Meg's feelings of stress over her workload decreased, her need to exercise so excessively also decreased. In equally small steps, Meg reduced her exercise time each night during the first week. During the second week, she decided to exercise only every other night (but for as long as she wanted) and to work out on the weekend if she felt like it. After six weeks of this gradual coping strategy, Meg found that when her boss said, "Meg, I want you to look this over tonight," she was able to stay calm. Two weeks after that she was able to load up her briefcase without the usual anxiety attacks that left her short of breath and with pounding heart. She also found that, although she did not exercise as frequently or intensely as before, she enjoyed her workouts a lot more because they were no longer driven by frustration and tension only. She was therefore able to fit in the number of workouts necessary to produce the health benefits exercise bestows—as well as keep up with her work.

Jack, too, followed the gradual approach to his dating problem. He also found that if he slowly and deliberately planned a dating situation, he was better able to handle the stress trigger, which he found to be fear of embarrassing himself. First he found a woman he wanted to date. Then he planned where he would take her. Then he decided how he would contact her and what he would say when he asked her. He made sure that the first date was an informal and short get-together at a place where he felt comfortable. The entire planning process took three weeks; the date was a thirty-minute lunch. Although Jack had to drag himself there with a lot of anticipated anxiety, he found that after an initial awkward period he was able to relax and actually enjoy himself. Jack continued to see this woman for gradually longer periods of time until he found that without giving it much thought his exercise time gradually diminished as his dating time increased.

Consider your problem. How can you take one small step toward dealing with it? Don't get ahead of yourself and worry about what the second and third and fourth steps will be because if you don't take the first, the rest is irrelevant. Don't move on until you're comfortable with that first small step. Combine this gradual approach with the stress-reduction techniques explained in Step Three and you'll soon find that each step forward is easier to take.

Step Three: Stress Management

It should not make you ashamed or embarrassed to find that you have stress triggers that are difficult for you to face. Stress is a part of everyone's life. Although you may admire the professional who never appears flustered or the politician who remains cool under pressure, even they are not immune to stress. They may be paying the price of hiding their stress responses with physical problems that can include ulcers, headaches, heart palpitations, and addictions, *or* they have learned how to manage them.

Steps One and Two have guided you through the first and most obvious parts of stress management by identifying, slowly confronting, and approaching (not avoiding) the stress trigger. While you are doing these things, you'll find that the inclusion of some of the following stress-management techniques will make it easier to get over the occasional bout with self-doubt and fear of failure.

Thought Reevaluation. The next time you find yourself confronting self-defeating thoughts, take some time to find out where they come from. People often give themselves a hard time because they don't stop and evaluate; they jump immediately into the reflexive reaction of beating themselves over the head. When you find yourself with thoughts like, "The boss must think I'm stupid or he wouldn't be so short with me," stop and reevaluate. Was he really short with just me, or is he short with everyone? Could there be other outside factors that didn't have anything to do with me? What type of pressure is he under? If you decide that you actually did do something wrong, stop and think again. Did I do it on purpose? Can I do it differently next time? Has anyone other than me ever made a mistake? What is the real consequence of that mistake?

If you tend to expand on the negative side of situations and dwell on it until it seems like the world will end, there are strategies that can help you lessen these catastrophic feelings. When you start to blow up a bad situation, remember to *stop* and *evaluate*. Evaluate the actual likelihood that each of the steps in your self-generated catastrophe will really happen. Will you, for example, really be demoted because the boss wanted a document set up differently? If you get demoted and take a pay cut, will you really have to stop eating at restaurants? If your pay is cut so much that you can't pay your rent, will you really have to move into a shelter? If you move into a shelter, where will you put the ironing board in order to keep your shirts pressed? Catastrophizing is intrinsically irrational—so is humor. You can limit your tendency to overemphasize the negative by trying to look at the bright side and by finding some humor in your exaggeration of potential consequences.

Deep Breathing. Since the body tends to respond to stress with altered breathing patterns, you can reduce or interrupt the stress you feel by regaining control of your breathing. Athletes often will do this just before a race begins or as they are about to get up to bat.

To stop the rapid breathing that accompanies a stress response:

• Put your hand on your stomach.
• Take a deep breath from the bottom of your stomach. Feel it fill you with air. Feel your hand rise with your stomach muscles.
• Breathe in as you silently count to five.
• Let the air go. Don't push it out. Let it go gently to the count of five.
• Do this sequence two times in a row.

• Then breathe again regularly, rhythmically, and comfortably.
• Deep breathe again after you have let a minute or two go by.
• Repeat this deep-breathing/regular-breathing cycle two or three times, or as often as needed, until you find your breathing has returned to a natural and comfortable pace.

Deep breathing is a strategy you can use anywhere. No one around needs to know you're practicing a stress-reduction technique, but you can employ it whenever you're feeling stressed.

Guided Imagery. Because we all daydream and night-dream, we already know we have an internal world that we can experience in both positive and negative ways. Guided imagery requires you to go to that inner world and imaginatively construct a place where you'll feel safe and relaxed whenever you picture yourself being there.

To do this, create a positive image in your mind that represents a safe and relaxing environment. Practice visiting it over and over again. Then when you are stressed, you can go there just briefly and benefit from the relaxed feeling it gives you.

For example, this is an image Jack found soothing: "I am sitting alone on a large flat rock on the shore of a lake in northern New Jersey. The morning sun is warm on my face and my sweater protects me from the breeze blowing off the water. Across the lake at the horizon I can see a few isolated cabins and the forest trees reaching toward a blue sky. I feel calm and peaceful. I have nothing pressing to do and nowhere important to go. There are no flies or mosquitos in my special place, nothing at all to cause me discomfort. It's an ideal place that I can visit with all my senses anytime I want. Even when I'm in the middle of a crowd with my eyes wide open, I can go to my place by the lake."

This safe place happens to be by a lake—yours can be anywhere. It can be in your family room by the fireplace, on the beach by the ocean, or in the park down the street. It can be anywhere, but there are certain things you should keep in mind:

• If you start to create your safe place and you find anything wrong (any elevation in SDs), take out the negative image. The possibilities of location are unlimited, so find an area that is *perfect.*

• Pick a familiar place that you find calm or soothing. This can be some place you've actually visited or one you've seen only in a book or movie, but when you're stressed, you won't be able to relate fully to an unfamiliar location.

• Involve all your senses. Make sure all the smells and the things you touch, taste, hear, and see in this environment are pleasing to you.

The more you practice the quality of your image, the more you can rely on it when you're stressed. It will become an overpracticed response.

Progressive Muscle Relaxation. In stressful situations many people describe the way they feel as being "tied up in knots." Because of the way our muscles react to stress, this is a good metaphor. Progressive muscle relaxation will enable you to untie those knots. Although we have the ability to relax our muscles, it is not something we often consciously do. By practicing progressive muscle relaxation you will learn what it feels like when stress begins to manifest itself in muscle tension. Then when your muscles tense in reaction to a real stress trigger, you will be able to identify the problem area and stop the stress attack.

To begin, tense and relax the various muscle groups listed below. Maintain that tension for fifteen seconds so you have time to feel how whole parts of your body are involved in tension. When you have a muscle group tensed, let your mind's eye experience that part of your body. If you're tensing your arm, for example, press your forearm down against the table. Feel where the tension goes out through your fingertips, up onto your shoulders, right into your neck—then relax. Consciously let go of the muscle tension.

Repeat the following exercise three times with these muscle groups:

1. right hand	make a fist
right forearm	press down
2. left hand	make a fist
left forearm	press down
3. shoulders	shrug
4. neck	lean your head back and roll it from side to side
5. head:	
jaw	bite down lightly
tongue	press on the roof of your mouth
eyes	squint
forehead	frown and raise your brows
6. abdomen	tighten your stomach as if someone were going to hit you
7. back	arch slightly
8. right leg	press down on the floor
left leg	press down on the floor
9. toes	curl under

There is no magic in this list of muscle groups. Pick ones that make sense for you and practice them until you're well acquainted with the feeling of tension in each one. Then give the method a chance to relieve the stress you feel in your life. The next time your SDs go over 50 and your muscles begin to tense, let your mind's eye go through your body to zero in on the location of the tension. For many people it's in the lower back, neck, or shoulders; for others it's in and around the forehead or the jaw area. When you've found your tense area, use the technique of progressive muscle relaxation to ease your discomfort.

The Three-Step Remedy explained above can solve avoidance dilemmas that are caused by feelings of tension, stress, and anxiety over fear of failure. There are other causes of avoidance, however, that reflect deeper issues in one's psychological makeup and that may require a more direct and focused approach to overcome; these include communication issues, poor time management, and significant lack of assertiveness. The suggested readings for this chapter in Appendix A will give you more information and further self-help readings on these subjects.

———

There is no doubt that exercise can help you avoid facing your problems. But as you certainly know, avoiding a problem doesn't make it go away; confronting a bad situation is the only way to master it. Exercise can keep you from dealing with life conflicts, but there are better strategies that can be used to confront the things you have been avoiding. Once you recognize the root of your addiction and ease yourself out of the excessive exercise program, you'll probably find that exercise in moderation can be used to help you deal with life's stresses in a positive way. Exercise can be useful when mastering a difficult situation and it can help build

3

Obsessive-Compulsive Exercisers

I do the same exercise routine every
day no matter what.

Thirty-two-year-old Janet is a legal secretary whose passion for an orderly daily schedule, a well-run office, and an efficient home-management system is a testament to her obsessive-compulsive personality; it is also the underlying root of her exercise addiction.

Like most people with obsessive-compulsive personality traits, Janet feels uncomfortable with any ambiguity or spontaneity and she feels that she needs structure in all aspects of her life in order to be comfortable. Her appointment calendar at work is carefully arranged to avoid schedule conflicts. Janet makes a daily checklist of things to do and crosses off each item when it is accomplished. Very concerned with nutrition, she plans her meals a week in advance and does her food shopping to fulfill this plan on Saturday at precisely two o'clock. Exercise time fits very neatly into this orderly, compartmentalized existence.

Janet recognizes her need for order, and in fact, has often turned it to her advantage; it's certainly her meticulous work habits that have in one year's time catapulted her to the position of office supervisor. But Janet does not recognize that because of her need for rigid scheduling she cannot enjoy any type of spontaneity. She could never, for example, set out for a weekend vacation without knowing exactly where she was going, what it would be like when she got there, and how she would spend her time until she returned. An impromptu adventure is not fun for people with obsessive-compulsive personalities.

Answer yes or no to the following questions. They will help you decide if your exercise addiction is rooted in obsessive-compulsive personality traits.

	YES	NO
1. Do you feel you need a certain amount or type of exercise, such as running at least three times per week, even though you know that you are getting enough exercise in other ways to stay in good shape and maintain your current level of proficiency?	____	____
2. Do you have a firm schedule for your workouts (as in *always* run one day and lift weights on another) and feel anxious if you need to switch days or skip an activity because of schedule, illness, or injury?	____	____
3. Are you uneasy when you can't exercise a predetermined amount (as in run exactly *five* miles and do *forty-five* minutes of aerobics) even if you *almost* get in that amount?	____	____
4. Do you feel particularly bad if you don't meet an exercise achievement		

goal (such as a seven-minute mile)
even if you try hard and have an
otherwise good workout?   ____ ____

5. Do you find that your performance
   often fails to meet the goals that you
   have set even if it has improved
   beyond its prior level?   ____ ____

6. Do you fulfill your preset exercise
   routine no matter how severe the
   weather or how pressured you are to
   fulfill other obligations?   ____ ____

The more often you answered yes to these questions, the
more likely it is that your personality has hooked you into
obsessive exercise routines.

THE PROBLEM

Although the need for a structured life-style may sound
uncomfortably regimented and negative to some, in Janet's
case she has been able to make her need for structure work
to her advantage. However, obsessive-compulsive traits are
potentially problematic in relation to exercise addiction: The
need for order is often accompanied by an attitude of perfectionism. If, for example, a schedule is not followed to the
minute, if a document is misplaced, or if an expectation of
personal accomplishment isn't met, perfectionists will suffer feelings of anxiety, dysphoria, and guilt and will frequently badger themselves with self-recriminations such as,
"You can't do anything right." People with these traits often
view the world in an all-or-nothing framework. Meeting 90
percent of a goal is no better than not meeting that goal at
all. In these cases, exercise can become the dose of orderly

activity that offers a crutch of immediate and predictable feedback, as well as the possibility for meeting 100 percent of a goal. Without exercise and the stability it provides, people with obsessive-compulsive traits can't maintain acceptable levels of positive emotional functioning.

An obsessive-compulsive *personality* is distinct from an obsessive-compulsive *disorder*. Most obsessive-compulsive personality types possess traits similar to Janet's. Clinically, they are characterized by a longstanding need for order and tendencies toward rigidity. They are perfectionists who can demonstrate unwavering perseverance along with a possible obstinate streak; they may also be emotionally restricted. Many of these traits seem to give them a sense of control that is a comfortable barrier against the terrors of chaos. When their expectations for structure aren't met their reactions will be marked by a vague sense of anxiety for which there is no well-understood physiological basis and which will usually not respond well to medication. Obsessive-compulsive personality traits are found equally in males and females. Those who use exercise as their crutch are typically latecomers to the exercise scene and often begin exercising in a very structured and single-minded way, trying to learn and master three new exercise routines at the same time. They may also devote extraordinary amounts of time to reading and talking about their chosen exercise. Obsessive-compulsive personality and its associated traits produce the kind of behavioral background that can lead to addiction.

Individuals with an obsessive-compulsive disorder (OCD), on the other hand, suffer from severe and chronic emotional problems characterized by intrusive and repetitive, often unpleasant, thoughts and/or ritualistic behavior patterns such as persistent hand washing, checking, or counting. People with an obsessive-compulsive disorder do not generally develop addictions to find relief from their problem; it is believed that affected persons have a biological imbalance that often can be effectively treated with medication or behavior therapy.*

As an obsessive-compulsive personality type, Janet does share some common characteristics with those having OCD. Both experience recurring self-doubt and indecisiveness. But while the person with OCD may relieve the anxiety of these feelings by engaging in highly repetitive, ritualistic acts or thoughts, those with obsessive-compulsive personality traits will most often attempt to ease their anxiety by finding something they can successfully organize and schedule. To do this many gravitate to exercise.

THE ADDICTION

Exercise offers individuals with obsessive-compulsive personality traits opportunities to ward off feelings of anxiety through a host of rigid and structured activities. Places like the track, the gym, the spa, or the pool are havens for those driven by a need to accomplish goals in an orderly fashion. They can set schedules that are inflexible and demanding. They know, in advance, what will happen for an extended period of time, so there are no surprises in their lives. Some will always set aside the hours between four and six on Saturdays to work out; others will plan to run on Sundays, perform an hour of aerobics on Mondays, play a tennis match on Tuesdays, run again on Wednesdays, and so on. Whether intensive or limited, once the exercise plan is set it

* A full description of the diagnostic criteria underlying OCP and OCD traits can be found in *Diagnostic and Statistical Manual of Mental Disorders* (3d rev. ed.).

is carved in stone; in this way obsessive-compulsives can use exercise to keep their calendars and, by extension, their lives neatly organized. And because exercise is an activity that can reap positive social support and even admiration, as well as manifest concrete and predictable improvement in things like musculature, technique, and timing, it can give them immediate positive feedback and an improved sense of self-esteem.

Like all rigid routines, exercise serves a specific function for obsessive-compulsive personalities. Generally these people have an inordinate need to be in control—no surprises, no variations in the original plan. They have to keep the upper hand over self and others and they fear impulses and spontaneous feelings. Naturally, they tend to pursue activities that guarantee, as far as is possible in life, absolute security and certainty. Exercise gives them all of these things. They can decide what kind of exercise to engage in, when to do it, and how long to do it. They can set goals and keep records. Janet never has to worry about where she'll be after work or what she'll do on the weekends, and she's never at the mercy of someone else's whim, because she knows she'll be exercising.

Janet practices three main types of exercise. She runs five days a week for five miles each time. On three of these days (always with a day in between) she does a full Nautilus circuit as well. On the other two days that she runs, Janet goes to the gym (always after work at around 5:30 P.M.) and does a Stairmaster workout for fifteen minutes. On her two nonrunning days, she goes to aerobics classes. If it should ever happen that Janet can't make it to these scheduled classes, she jumps rope for a half hour.

Exercise lets Janet be in charge. If you take away her scheduled exercise period, you take away her sense of self-control. Exercise functions as her base of security.

Second, exercise enables people with this type of personality to mask their perceived inadequacies. Because these types strive so relentlessly for perfection, it is quite common for them to feel inadequate and incompetent in social, family, and/or work situations. These feelings are temporarily eased by a retreat to the concrete and predictable world of exercise. An exercise schedule is something they can develop with competency, use to set attainable goals, and manipulate to satisfy their need for perfection. Janet is in charge of fifteen legal assistants, most of whom are older and more experienced than she. Her workdays are filled with self-doubt; she continually worries that one day her inexperience will cost her her job. Janet works hard to reduce her chronic sense of inadequacy by exercising; for her this is an activity that gives her complete control of her life without a moment of self-doubt. She can increase the weight she lifts on the Nautilus machines, increase the difficulty of the Stairmaster, or increase the level of her aerobics class. All of this adds to her sense of mastery and competency.

Finally, obsessive-compulsive personalities find it easier to ignore feelings of anxiety and dissatisfaction when they are wrapped up in an obsessive endeavor like exercise. These individuals, who suffer recurring bouts of depression, stress, or anxiety, will generally handle their problems in one of two ways. They may decide to discover why they feel as they do, face their problems and work on them to improve the quality of their lives. Or, like most exercise addicts, they may try to ignore and deny them. Exercise routines are structured and time-consuming; they leave little opportunity to think about one's state of mental health. Organizing an exercise session can take a lot of time and effort: The exerciser must plan the regimen, get to the exercise place, engage in the activity, wash up afterward, and return home. Obsessive-compulsive exercisers often keep complex and meticulous records of their workouts, which occupies even more of their time.

While exercise efficiently serves the emotional needs of many people with obsessive-compulsive personality traits, it does not solve the underlying problems; instead it tends to compound them by hiding the root of the anxiety and by heaping on the additional burdens inherent in all addictions. While putting in the time and effort to organize and carry out exercise programs, the feelings of anxiety and depression are temporarily relieved. But like all other addictions, as soon as the activity is stopped, the feelings return and the individual needs another, and soon more potent, "fix" in order to maintain the accustomed level of normal functioning.

One evening Janet was detained by a business meeting that ran late. She had planned to run five miles and then do the Nautilus circuit. She knew that if she stayed at the meeting, her exercise schedule would be ruined. Janet could feel her initial sense of vague annoyance rapidly growing into intense anxiety. As the meeting continued ("dragged on," in her opinion), she found herself becoming more anxious and depressed. Soon in an absolute panic, Janet abruptly excused herself and fled the meeting for the gym, justifying her actions by reminding herself that she had worked hard all day and had carefully planned a good workout; no one had a right to change those plans.

What Janet didn't know was that her desire for exercise had nothing to do with employee rights or earned rewards; it grew from a more personal source. Her obsessive-compulsive behavior led her to feel that if her exercise plans were changed, she would lose control of her life. If she lost control, she would feel vulnerable to her low self-esteem.

She felt that without this "fix" her incompetence would affect her ability to do her job. However, an objective view of the situation makes it clear that if Janet's job is in jeopardy, it is because of her lack of flexibility, not a lack of skills. Janet will be a poor candidate for further promotions that involve more work time, travel, spontaneous meetings, responsibilities, and so on, because like most obsessive-compulsive personalities, under stress Janet will seek a more, not less, rigid schedule. Ironically, Janet is hurting herself professionally by using exercise to make herself feel better about her work situation. Abruptly leaving a meeting has the potential to do more harm to Janet's career than any possible work deficiencies caused by her imagined lack of competence; however, she knew only that she *had* to leave. Despite her planning and organizing, Janet is not really in control. She is using exercise as a strategy to organize and occupy her time, unaware of its potential for significantly negative consequences.

Another common scenario that illustrates the problems with an obsessive-compulsive personality–based exercise addiction is found in the single woman or man who, like Janet, needs to work out even when this interferes with other goals. Although possibly very lonely and longing to meet a "significant other," these exercise addicts will go to the gym each night after work; refuse social opportunities that might keep them up late and hurt their next day's workout; and essentially, in spite of the desire to meet someone special, lock themselves into a world comprised of work and exercise with no time for anything else. For them, exercise provides an arena where they can feel competent and elevate their self-esteem, and it gives them a "valid" excuse for avoiding dating and social situations where they may often feel inadequate.

If an obsessive-compulsive type deprived of scheduled exercise cannot function with peace of mind or feel an adequate sense of self-worth, he or she is addicted. This person needs to realize that exercise is not relieving anxieties; it's only masking them.

THE REMEDY

As you try to reduce your dependency on your addiction, remember that the goal is not to give up exercise but to become more flexible about when, how often, and in what way you exercise. Once you meet this goal, you will be able to function at your accustomed level of proficiency without becoming upset if your exercise routine should be interrupted by an appointment, illness, or injury.

During this period of readjustment you'll also need to examine your attitudes about exercise. Exercise should be an enjoyable activity that you do when you can, not an intense, all-absorbing chore you feel you must do even when you can't conveniently make the time. When you do this, you'll be using exercise for the healthy and positive benefits it has to offer rather than as a means to avoid thinking about painful and difficult feelings.

If you have an obsessive-compulsive–based exercise addiction you know that you cannot simply decide to stop using exercise as a space filler and organizer for your schedule. Because of the way you approach situations you will need to know what you will be doing each day and you won't be comfortable with a trial-and-error kick-the-habit program. So take the following suggestions in the order they're given and apply them to your exercise routine *gradually.*

CHANGE THE TIMING OF YOUR EXERCISE SCHEDULE

The first step in adding some flexibility to your exercise routine is to change the exercise schedule itself. You could continue doing the same exercise routine at the same level of intensity and for the same duration of time but simply change the time when you do it. If, for example, you usually exercise on Monday, Wednesday, Friday, and Saturday, try changing your Saturday time to Sunday.

Once you take this small step you can begin to do more extensive scrambling. Each week switch your exercise period around to different days because if you make the Saturday to Sunday switch permanent, you've simply created a new rigid schedule. The goal is to feel free to plan a new schedule each week and flexibly fit exercise into your life.

How long you should do this before moving on to the next schedule change depends on how long it takes you to feel comfortable with the first step. If you find it quite easy to change exercise days, move right along. If, however, you feel anxious about the switching of days even after one month, you're probably not ready to move on. Adjusting to flexibility (even when you're structuring it) is difficult for some obsessive-compulsive personalities. You must give yourself as much time as you need to accept the "routine" of changing routines.

If you exercise every day, or if your life schedule is so tight there is no room for any kind of switching, this initial step won't be effective for you. That's okay; jump ahead to the next step.

Once you can change your exercise days with ease, try changing the length of time you exercise. In small increments, change your two-hour workout to a one and a half–

hour one. You can do this by quitting earlier or by changing the starting time. If you usually start your session at 7:00, start at 7:30 instead.

Don't do this every day, just once in a while. Teach your internal timekeeper that you won't suffer if you miss a few minutes of exercise time. This will be easier to do if you keep in mind the body's physical needs rather than your psychological ones. (While changing the duration of your exercise time, you should continue to move around your exercise days.)

While *change* is the key to breaking an addiction that is expressed in an obsessive-compulsive personality style, scheduling that change is the key to its success. Don't move your exercise day from Saturday to Sunday and leave Saturday with nothing to do. This would surely doom your attempts because the need for a schedule is still a part of your makeup; work with that fact, not against it. In the same way, if you move the time period from 7:00 to 7:30, fill in that preempted half hour with something else! Sitting in the locker room waiting out your schedule change is looking for failure. With a positive attitude schedule a quick shopping trip, a visit with a friend, or some overtime at work. As you slowly take away from your exercise time, carefully plan to fill in the spaces with other constructive activities.

One last word of advice as you plan to implement this first step: The more difficult you find it to change your exercise schedule in these small, simple steps, the more determined you should be. Don't feel defeated by this; use it to bolster your conviction. Because of the way you look at the world, you are typically concerned with doing things right; let this work in your favor by making the implementation of a flexible schedule a self-improvement goal that you want to achieve.

CHANGE YOUR EXERCISE GOALS

As you make your schedule more flexible, you can also begin to change the way you view the role of exercise in your life. Rather than using it as an activity that allows you to continue your struggle toward perfectionism, slowly begin to use it for enjoyment and physical health. As an obsessive-compulsive personality you most likely keep track of your workouts. You time yourself, count your miles, laps and repetitions, and set personal goals that challenge you to do more and better. This need to excel and to keep up with past performances is reasonable, but lack of flexibility fuels the problem you have with exercise.

Look at other areas of your life where you feel it is crucial to be perfect. For the time being, keep the focus of your perfectionistic drive on these areas, which may include work, family, and social organizations. But plan to drop exercise from the list. Put it in a category called "recreation"—nothing more and nothing less. Also plan to give this change of focus plenty of time to take hold. It's taken quite a while for your addiction to develop; give yourself at least several weeks to shift your need for rigid scheduling to some other activity.

When you're comfortable with this idea, slowly eliminate record keeping from your workouts. Stop counting, recording, timing, and pacing. Instead of planning to run for five miles, for example, plan to run for forty-five minutes. During this time, don't count—enjoy the scenery or just the movement of your body itself. Give it a try. Can you enjoy exercise without setting performance goals? Can you do a Nautilus workout without recording the weight and repetitions? Can you go for a long, fun bike ride without noting how far you went and how long it took? Yes, of course, part of the purpose of many exercise activities is to compete and improve performance, but it is only *part*. During this phase of the remedy, slowly strive to take the full and intense focus off self-competition and put it on enjoyment and physical fitness. You can always reintroduce those self-competitive elements that you want and feel you can control.

CHANGE YOUR MODE OF EXERCISE

Don't panic at the suggestion of changing your form of exercise. If you love running or aerobics or weight lifting or tennis, and so on, you should continue to do these things. But to break the hold of your addiction, you should delegate some of your exercise time to a variety of physical activities. In this way you'll be combining flexibility of time with flexibility of activity in a scheduled, well-planned manner that should not throw your need for order into a tizzy.

Plan to bicycle instead of run next Saturday. Or plan to swim instead of dance on Wednesday. Or plan to walk instead of doing calisthenics on Monday. As soon as you attempt to do this, you may find yourself defensively questioning why you should give up something you know you enjoy for something you're not interested in. The answer is as complex as the addiction itself, but basically you'll find that the change in activity is also a change in the environmental and social triggers that feed your obsession with exercise. New forms of recreation will pull you away from intense self-focus, yet still give you outlets for physical movement.

If you are occasionally able to substitute one form of exercise for another, you'll be more able to kick the habit. New modes of exercise will keep your schedule intact, will fill in the time frame allotted for exercise, and will continue to foster physical fitness, but will simultaneously weaken the addictive holds of tolerance, cravings, dependence, and avoidance of withdrawal. It's also true that altering exercise routines, or cross-training as it is often called, is known to be healthy for you and your muscles; in fact, elite athletes now recognize this and vary their exercise in order to improve their primary-sport performance.

Nonaddicted exercisers are able to adjust to changes in exercise plans because they can substitute. If the weather cancels a planned outdoor run, they can adapt to the situation and swim some laps instead. If a schedule problem keeps weight lifters away from the gym, they can do some at-home calisthenics or jump rope. If tennis elbow keeps players off the courts, they can bicycle, run, or swim, without suffering the withdrawal pains of canceled games.

It's very easy for an obsessive-compulsive–based exerciser to become so caught up in training and competing that he or she loses all sense of enjoyment from the sport. That's why it's not uncommon for addicted exercisers who change exercise modes to discover that they don't really miss anything about their former exercise. It becomes just one more area where they need to struggle to achieve for the sake of self-esteem. If you can gradually introduce new forms of exercise into your schedule, you'll find that you won't be so dependent on your exercise of choice; this, of course, weakens the addiction and frees you to enjoy exercise for its health-promoting benefits. Knowing you can make up the session some other time or can substitute some other activity even after the gym, spa, courts, pool, and so on close also lessens your fear of schedule interference. Cross-training also offers a health advantage in that, because it uses varying sets of muscles, the exerciser is less prone to the injuries so common in the one-sport addict.

If you find you cannot adjust to the changes suggested above, even after very gradual, unpressured, yet deliberate attempts, you should consider that your obsessive-compulsive personality has a stronger grasp on your life functioning than can be remedied in self-help fashion. People with significant obsessive-compulsive traits can be treated with psychotherapy. It is often true that working with a therapist who understands the way you think can reduce the tendencies toward rigidity that drive your personality. Often the regular contact and encouragement received from a therapist can help you to recognize and cope with some of the things that are impossible to work out without help.

4

Depression and Anxiety States

Exercise is the only thing that
makes me feel normal.

For many people suffering from transient mild to moderate depression or anxiety, the benefits of exercise are substantial enough to recommend it as the treatment of first choice. There are several characteristics for evaluating the successful use of therapeutic exercise. These include:

1. *Rapid response.* If exercise makes you feel better right from the first time or two you use it, it is more likely to be helpful.

2. *Sense of enjoyment.* If you enjoy the exercise activity and feel comfortable with it, it is more likely to be a useful tactic.

3. *Duration of effect.* If you feel better for an extended period, like the rest of the day (or even for two or more days) per workout, the promise for maximum benefit is heightened.

4. *Benefits at low doses.* If you tend to feel relief from your negative mood state even when you work out for only short periods, exercise is more likely to be a positive mood enhancer for you.

It's important to keep in mind, however, that persistent depression or anxiety is not always best treated with exercise alone. Although exercise may provide temporary relief for mild, moderate, and even severe depressed moods, there are many cases when it fails to make the symptoms and problems go away completely. Even in these cases, exercise may provide a temporary benefit. The problem is that symptoms are partially or temporarily reduced but not eliminated. Therefore, because exercise has the potential to reduce symptoms temporarily without effectively eliminating them it also has the potential to create a dependence without providing a cure.

Do you exercise excessively to hide a problem with depression or anxiety? The following quiz will help you decide.

	YES	NO
1. Do you find that exercise improves your mood by either reducing anxiety or lessening depression?	____	____
2. Do you feel lethargic or tense until you exercise each day?	____	____
3. Do you find that you need to exercise more now than when you began exercising to get the same improvement in your mood?	____	____
4. Do you find that the elevation in your mood you get from exercising occurs for a shorter and shorter period each time?	____	____
5. Do you find that your mood is better only while you are exercising?	____	____
6. Do you need to increase the duration or intensity of your exercise in order to get the same effect on your mood or to		

have the effect last as long as it used to
with less exercise?   ____ ____

7. Do you find that it takes longer and
   longer to warm up when you start to
   exercise—that you feel stiff or
   lethargic for longer each time?   ____ ____

8. Do you find that your mood is worse
   than ever when you can't exercise?   ____ ____

9. Does the idea of missing exercise
   increase your depression or anxiety?   ____ ____

If you answer yes to the majority of these questions, your
attempt to self-treat a mood disorder with exercise is falling
short of an effective remedy. This chapter will help you
understand how moods can react to exercise and then help
you find an appropriate place for exercise in your efforts to
maintain a sense of well-being.

To understand exercise addiction with its roots in depression and anxiety states, we first need to define exactly what
is meant by these terms.*

DEPRESSION

We all know what depression is. We have each suffered
through times when we feel sad and listless; sometimes
these feelings are combined with a drop in self-esteem and a
sense of "Who cares?" Fortunately for most of us, these
feelings fade after a while and life becomes worth living
again. Because for many others these feelings do not fade,
depression is probably the most common form of psycho-
pathology. Depression has specific characteristics and is

---

* The medical descriptions and diagnostic information in this chapter are based
on standards presented in *Diagnostic and Statistical Manual of Mental Disorders*
(3d rev. ed).

clinically divided into two catagories: major depression and dysthymic disorder.

Major depression is the most severe type of depressive disorder. It is characterized by feelings of sadness or loss of interest in pleasurable activities for at least a two- to four-week period. In addition, the depressed person suffers other symptoms that include disturbances in sleep, appetite, interest, and activity levels. Strictly speaking it is not a genetic illness but it is thought to run in families.

Many exercise-addicted runners experience the classic symptoms of major depression when deprived of their exercise for an extended period of time by such unavoidable factors as injury or illness. However, it is uncommon that the major-depressive episode would lead to exercise addiction. People suffering this mood disorder are often too tired and dysfunctional to exercise excessively. Though the anxiety and depression that come from an interruption in an exercise schedule could trigger a major depression in certain people, exercise will offer only temporary relief for the problem. Exercise can be reinforcing to many who have depressed moods but not to those with major depressions, because the many other symptoms related to major depression would persist no matter how much one exercised.

Dysthymic disorder, on the other hand, is an extremely common, milder form of depression that more readily lends itself to exercise addiction. Dysthymia (also called depressive neurosis) is a chronic mood disturbance that causes a person to feel unhappy more often than not. This disorder usually begins in childhood, adolescence, or early adulthood. Because chronic unhappiness can become a part of an affected person's view of life, it is also often referred to as depressive personality. There is evidence that this disorder is more common among parents, children, and siblings of people with major depression than among the general population and is seemingly more common in females. The average age of onset is about thirty for men and forty for women. It can, however, also develop in children and the elderly. Unlike some other psychiatric disorders, like schizophrenia, depression is found among members of all social classes.

If you suspect that your exercise addiction is rooted in depression, use the following dysthymia checklist to help you zero in on your problem. Answer yes or no as you would respond if you were *not* exercising.

DYSTHYMIA CHECKLIST

	YES	NO
1. Do you feel sad most of the day, more days than not?	___	___
2. During these depressed periods do you notice at least two of the following: a. poor appetite or overeating? b. insomnia or excessive sleeping? c. low energy or fatigue? d. low sense of self-esteem? e. poor concentration or difficulty making decisions? f. feelings of hopelessness?	___	___
3. In the last two years, have you never been without the above symptoms for more than two months at a time?	___	___
4. Are you now and in the past have you been suffering from chronic psychotic disorders such as schizophrenia or delusional disorder?	___	___
5. Are you certain there is no organic factor (such as the use of antihypertensive medication) causing your feelings of sadness?	___	___

If you answered yes to all five of these questions, most likely you are suffering from mild yet chronic depression. In that case it would not be uncommon for the disorder to be a possible cause of a variety of problems, including the development of an exercise addiction.

Paul is a thirty-five-year-old unmarried dentist who, although professionally and financially successful, uses exercise to mask his depression. Paul has no trouble finding a date when he wants to, has many acquaintances, and has some old college friends, but he is often alone and depressed about his lack of a social life. Paul has had girlfriends, but these relationships rarely lasted more than three or four months, and now he no longer dates much at all. Paul says this is because he hasn't found many women who appeal to him, and also because he likes to get to sleep early in order to feel full of energy for his daily early-morning workout.

Paul excels at two sports: cycling and running; he has recently even competed in a few biathlons. Paul cycled throughout his college days, did well academically, and had an active social life. Work rewards him financially and intellectually, and Paul enjoys his job, but in the last seven years he has grown somewhat moody. During this past year, Paul has found cycling more and more rewarding, and he has noticed that his moodiness often lifts after a workout and that sometimes the high-spirited feeling remains for a while afterward. He has even joined a cycling club and has begun running. Paul now puts a lot of energy into both sports. His four mornings a week of cycling or running have gradually expanded to six or seven; this keeps Paul in a fairly good mood for the early part of the day. But by evening he often feels lonely and depressed again, so he began going for short nighttime workouts four to seven times a week. Again, he's noticed that his spirits are higher after this second workout.

Paul now adds an occasional weekend race to this schedule as well, so he rarely has time to think about being lonely or depressed.

Paul has gradually, and unwittingly, built an exercise program to control his moodiness. Because his excessive exercise schedule so effectively offsets his chronic, low-level depression, he is most unwilling to give up a workout. His fear of feeling down has compelled him to work his dental practice around his exercise needs and all but eliminate his social life. Although at the present moment, exercise is helping Paul avoid feeling depressed, in the long run it may compound his social problems, intensifying the potential for severe depression and keeping him from dealing directly with the real problem. In this kind of scenario, exercise is working against, rather than toward, the attainment of mental health.

ANXIETY

Anxiety encompasses a wide range of human feelings— from a student's sense of alarm before a big test to a senior citizen's unprovoked panic attack in the supermarket that leads to hospitalization for a cardiac problem. Because we all experience feelings of anxiety from time to time, it's important to understand the kind of anxiety state that most commonly fosters obsessive exercise habits. That form of anxiety is called generalized anxiety disorder.

Generalized anxiety disorder (GAD) is characterized by unfocused and unrealistic or excessive anxiety and worry that is unrelated to any psychotic, eating, anxiety, or depressive disorder. Although the age of onset is variable, it most commonly begins in the twenties (sometimes after a major-depressive episode) and often continues for many years. The disorder may follow a familial pattern and is equally common in males and females. If you feel worried, anxious, or tense more often than not, answer the following questions to help you determine if these uneasy feelings may in fact be an anxiety disorder that has pushed you into exercise abuse.

ANXIETY DISORDER CHECKLIST

Put a check (√) next to each symptom you experience frequently.

Motor tension
__ 1. trembling, twitching, or feeling shaky
__ 2. muscle tension, aches, or soreness
__ 3. restlessness
__ 4. easy fatigability

Autonomic hyperactivity
__ 1. shortness of breath or smothering sensations
__ 2. palpitations or accelerated heart rate
__ 3. dry mouth
__ 4. dizziness or light-headedness
__ 5. nausea, diarrhea, or other abdominal distress
__ 6. hot flashes or chills
__ 7. frequent urination
__ 8. trouble swallowing or "lump in throat"

Vigilance and scanning
__ 1. feeling keyed up or on edge
__ 2. exaggerated startle response
__ 3. difficulty concentrating or "mind going blank" because of anxiety
__ 4. trouble falling or staying asleep
__ 5. irritability

If you find you have at least three to five checks on this inventory list and know that your anxiety is not caused by an organic factor such as hyperthyroidism or caffeine intoxication, it is likely that your need to exercise excessively is rooted in anxiety or in a diagnosable case of generalized anxiety disorder. Any one of these symptoms is unpleasant to experience. Whether or not they meet all of the criteria of GAD, people who regularly experience any of these symptoms often seek outside remedies. It is not uncommon for these people to overuse drugs or alcohol to cope with anxiety symptoms—others use exercise.

Although depression and anxiety are two different mood states, in many ways they are similar in their function as roots of exercise addiction. The following discussions apply equally to exercise addictions based in either depression or anxiety states.

THE ADDICTION

Exercise is good therapy for some people with negative mood disorders; for others it is ineffective and even counterproductive. The line between effective self-treatment and addiction is drawn at the point where the depressed or anxious person becomes dependent on exercise while trying to maintain an acceptable degree of mood functioning.

Both dysthymia and anxiety symptoms affect a person's mood "more often than not." Many people suffering these maladies find that exercise can tip this imbalance and allow them to experience positive feelings (particularly in the self-esteem dimension) more frequently than not. Unfortunately, in many cases the lift generated by exercise is short-lived and the exercise routine must soon be repeated to maintain or regain the mood elevation. Thus, an addictive cycle begins.

Your body develops a tolerance for the amount of exercise that you initially found eased the impact of a mood disorder. Quite naturally, there is a tendency to increase the intensity, duration, and frequency of the exercise program to maintain the same level of benefits. As your body becomes conditioned to expect more intense workouts, the positive effects have the potential to become shorter-lived (sometimes lasting no longer than the time of the actual workout). This is when cravings can develop and you'll find that your exercise routine takes precedence over things that were formerly more important. Once exercise achieves this priority status, your positive moods may become dependent upon a workout.

For a long time, you may feel that the energy and time spent working out is worth all that must be given up for it. It's a trade-off that makes sense as long as the workouts remain less in control of your life than your former misery was. After a while, however, the previously contented exerciser can no longer find the same lift and needs to increase the intensity, duration, or even frequency of the exercise session. Soon the workouts will cause as much distress as the former negative moods and the trade-off will become unacceptable.

Some exercise addicts exercise excessively in the mistaken belief that continuous exercise can prevent the occurrence of future episodes of depression or anxiety. Although there is no evidence that this is possible, it's easy to understand that exercisers might superstitiously cling to their regimens in the belief that they are warding off unpleasant experiences. Certainly if you found that in the past exercise was able to ease the affects of depression or anxiety, you might get caught up in the fear that if you stop exercising you'll risk a return of the problem. And so you'd unknowingly instigate a case of exercise addiction to accommodate this faulty belief.

Some excessive exercisers, especially runners, have heard via the grapevine that intense long-distance running relieves negative moods by giving the body and mind a boost through aerobic-based release of endorphins, opiatelike substances found in the brain that can produce the same euphoric and pain-relieving effects as externally administered opiates. Many excessive exercisers believe there is a linear relationship between amount of exercise, release of endorphins, and degree of depression and anxiety relief. The longer you run, some believe, the greater the mood elevation will be. However, this theory does not hold up scientifically.

New studies have found a simpler relationship between exercise and mood improvement. One research team discovered that both running and nonaerobic activities such as weight lifting, equivalent only to a college physical education class, offer an equivalently marked positive mood change. Apparently it is not the kind or degree of exercise that fosters mood improvement but simply the ability of participants to conceptualize themselves as exercisers. In fact, the extent to which participation actually alters the level of a person's self-esteem and mood is not related to the extent of improved aerobic fitness levels. Thus, harder work doesn't necessarily mean a better mood. When people engage in activity that is socially acceptable and positive, they feel good about themselves just because they do it.

The downside of this discovery is that it makes mood-related exercise addiction a more likely possibility in a wider range of exercise modes than was originally thought. As exercisers of all types can find mood alteration in small doses of almost any physical activity, they may arrive at the faulty conclusion that "If a little is good, a lot will be better." And so they double their exercise time seeking double benefits. Because the positive results can be short-lived, the exercisers may return to the specific activity more and more frequently. They find out too late that, as with other addictive substances and activities, more is not better.

THE PROBLEM

The problem with using exercise as a means of mood elevation is that its short-term positive effects cloud its overall long-term ineffectiveness. Yes, exercise can relieve the impact of depression and anxiety in many people and leave them relatively free of these mood disorders, but for many others, the positive effects of exercise kick in rapidly but last for no more than an hour. If the severity of the depression or anxiety is significant enough or persistent enough, the negative feelings will reappear as soon as the exercise session is over, or even begin to intrude into the exercise session itself. Thus, repeated frequent doses of intense exercise will be required to reduce the emotional symptoms adequately.

What happens to your mood when you don't get your exercise fix? If you have found that your mood problem is relieved by exercise, you may have increased the duration and frequency of your workouts to gain greater psychological benefits. You may have also found that when you are not exercising your moods are still negative and that you have forfeited a great deal in terms of social, occupational, family, and personal interests in your efforts to treat your mood problem. Most likely, you have learned that exercise is not a long-term solution for depression or anxiety states.

Even in the best-case scenario, in which exercise is used successfully to treat negative moods, exercise is not always a complete cure. Research data suggest that exercise has its primary effect on self-esteem or self-image. Thus, exercise may not alleviate the secondary problems, such as insomnia, loss of appetite, or poor concentration. So although some individuals are still suffering to some degree, exercise might keep them from seeking and implementing additional and alternate methods of mood management that, when combined with moderate exercise, have persistently shown positive results. These include medication, psychotherapy, relaxation techniques, and stress-management strategies. By ignoring other avenues of help, some people who are self-treating depression or anxiety with exercise are reducing their chances for a full recovery. This, of course, endangers their capacity for full psychological functioning in the future.

Dan is a thirty-year-old account executive with a large mail-order firm who suffers from an exercise addiction caused by anxiety. A year ago, he sought psychiatric help after his medical internist couldn't find an organic cause for his recurring episodes of muscle aches, general fatigue, dizziness, pounding heart, insomnia, and irritability. He had initially thought that he had a heart condition of some type. But he was eventually diagnosed as having generalized anxiety disorder and began psychotherapy to address his incessant worrying about things that most probably would never happen.

During this time, Dan's wife, too, was eager to help him regain a sense of calm. When she saw him start to show signs of anxiety, she would encourage him to join her in a jog around the lake because she had heard that running was an effective relaxation technique. Initially, Dan was less than enthusiastic about this idea. He had never been much of an athlete; his exercising had been limited to college intramurals and an occasional picnic softball or volleyball game. "I've told you," he'd complain, "that my muscles hurt and that I'm tired and dizzy. You don't understand if you think I should get up and run." But later, Dan's therapist also suggested exercise as a possible source of relief, so Dan gave it a try the next time he found himself falling victim to another round of useless, worrisome thoughts.

After his first few runs around the lake, Dan was delighted to find that for the first time in more than two years he could short-circuit his anxiety attacks with a ten- to twenty-minute run. It was as if someone had handed him a miracle cure. At his next session, Dan explained his new plan of attack to his therapist. "If I run every morning," he reasoned, "I shouldn't have any more problems with anxiety, and hopefully"—he smiled to show he meant no offense—"I won't be seeing you much longer."

The following week, Dan returned to report his progress. "I felt great every day after running before work; now I'm planning to add more distance each day because I figure the longer I run, the more benefit I'll gain. At work I still start to feel light-headed and tense so I'm thinking about running at lunchtime too. This is great," Dan beamed. "No drugs, no therapy, no problems, *and* I'm getting back into good shape!"

Eventually, Dan canceled all appointments with his therapist, and the therapist heard nothing more from Dan until seven months later when he called the office after suffering an intense anxiety attack. As the story unfolded, Dan explained that until two weeks earlier he had been running each morning and evening. He used this exercise routine to ward off anxiety and found it so vital to his mental health that he put aside other priorities and obligations he would otherwise have fulfilled in those time periods he now rigidly devoted to exercise.

Dan had developed a tolerance for his original quick runs, so he needed to add additional miles to gain the same physical and mental benefits. He also found himself craving his runs and canceling family and business appointments to satisfy the urge and to calm his fears. Then he fell down a flight of stairs while moving some boxes into the attic. Dan hurt his left knee and couldn't run for at least a month.

Because Dan's ability to function normally had become dependent on exercise he was now experiencing a return of his anxiety symptoms. His original problem with anxiety gradually returned along with an abrupt onset of difficulties associated with the compounding addiction problems. "I feel so sluggish," he confessed. "I have no appetite; I can't sleep; my head hurts, and I feel useless and angry. What's happening? I feel worse now than I did when I first came to you!" Dan returned to his therapist for an answer to his question and also because he had lost the support of his family and friends who had become tired of coming in second to exercise and didn't want to hear his complaining now that he had to spend more time at home. Dan had temporarily lost the external mechanism that enabled him to feel good about himself. Without exercise, Dan had lost his "cure" for anxiety, his self-esteem, and his ability to function in the manner necessary to his work and personal life.

In moderate amounts, exercise could have helped Dan deal with his problems and given him enough time and objectivity to seek additional forms of help. Unfortunately, Dan, like many others who use exercise to self-treat anxiety or depression, fell hard for the idea that more is better. Now Dan and his therapist had to find a way to help him use alternate types of exercise that could be practiced with a bad knee; Dan had to ease himself into a program that would reduce the frequency of exercise and maintain his self-esteem. Dan and his therapist had to return to the original problem of his mood disorder and start again to look for a way to help him function calmly and happily.

THE REMEDY

Exercise is a natural mood elevator, and we recommend it as a way to cope with the inevitable stresses of daily living; however, it should not be used as the sole method of treatment for moderate to severe cases of depression or anxiety. Therefore, the remedy for exercisers who have become addicted through their attempts to mask these emotional problems lies in taking steps to reduce the frequency and intensity of the exercise regimens while finding new ways to reduce the impact of anxious or depressed moods.

CHANGING YOUR EXERCISE SCHEDULE

The first step in redirecting the addict's use of exercise from negative to positive is to create a new exercise schedule. Many people suffering anxiety disorders or dysthymia schedule their workouts in response to their moods. They'll exercise with great urgency when they have a bad day at work or begin to feel lonely or tense. To prevent this, you should make up a weekly exercise schedule that allows for workouts only at predetermined times. (This remedy is obviously quite different from the one for exercisers whose dependence is rooted in obsessive-compulsive tendencies.)

When you do exercise at your scheduled time, make sure the intensity level of your workout doesn't exceed your body's maximum capacity. There is no reason in a healthy exercise program (the kind you are now trying to develop) to push yourself to the point of extreme breathlessness, cramps, and fatigue. The physical and emotional benefits of exercise are attained at a much lower level of intensity than many addicts are accustomed to using.

If you presently exercise two or more times a day, you'll find that reducing the frequency of workouts in your exercise schedule will also aid in your efforts to normalize your fitness program. You can gradually reduce your sessions so ultimately you exercise at most once a day. When you're comfortable with this schedule (or if you already exercise only once a day) begin to skip an occasional day. Remember that the goal of this step is to reduce the amount of time you feel you *must* dedicate to your workouts.

Although you may feel committed to your particular mode of exercise, be it running, cycling, walking, golfing, and so on, you will find that you can continue to exercise and take positive steps toward helping your mood disorder by switching to a different form of exercise, at least once a week, that involves contact with other people. If, for example, you usually lift weights and run, try a partner sport like tennis, squash, or racquetball. Or if you cycle, walk, or swim, join an aerobics class, play pickup basketball games, or find an exercise partner. This will give your exercise time the two desired remedy components of positive contact with others and the physical outlet of exercise.

As you make these changes in your exercise schedule, monitor your moods. Although you may initially experience a period of exercise withdrawal that can involve increased negative mood symptoms, after a month it is possible that the reduction in exercise frequency and intensity will not increase the occurrence of negative mood states at all. Appropriately scheduled and executed exercise will still give you the desired benefit of an improved sense of well-being. It will not, however, change the fact that you have a mood disorder. Read chapter 7 (page 129) carefully so you understand how the maximum benefits of exercise are achieved at a normalized baseline state even though you may feel that this schedule leaves you far short of a "perfect" mood.

SELF-TREATMENT OF MOOD DISORDERS

As you begin to organize a more normal exercise schedule, you'll need to fill the preempted time spaces with activities that will help you deal constructively with your anxiety or depression.

If you suffer from anxiety, there are numerous alternate means of reducing your tension. You might spend time practicing the progressive-muscle and guided-imagery exercises explained on page 42 in chapter 2. Many find relief through meditation, listening to music, or reading.

Dysthymics should also use a portion of their former exercise time to find an alternate means of self-directed mood elevation. Just as you put time and energy into an exercise program to boost your moods, you can now ease your symptoms by combining exercise with pleasant activities that involve seeing other people (not avoiding them as many exercise addicts often do). Don't leave enjoyable experiences to chance; schedule them on your weekly calendar by directing your social life toward fun things like eating out, dancing, visiting museums or parks. If you have children, spend more time with them and let yourself enjoy their company. See Appendix A for a list of books that offer self-help treatment for anxiety and depression.

By changing your schedule, you call into play a variety of mood enhancers. You'll still have your regular mode of exercise, mixed with new forms of physical activity that incorporate more contact with other people; in addition you'll have more time to practice techniques and strategies that have been proven helpful in easing the symptoms of mood disorders.

If, however, after a month or two your new self-treatment program is not helping you balance your moods, you may find greater relief with professional help. In most cases, psychotherapy and/or medication are effective means of treating the mood disorders of generalized anxiety disorder and dysthymia.

5

Body-Image Problem Exercisers

I'm going to look like the model in this magazine if it kills me.

BODY IMAGE

Would it surprise you to learn that many of today's American women cringe when they look at their naked bodies, or that some even avoid ever looking in a full-length mirror? Probably not. Dissatisfaction with one's body is common because so few possess the tall and slim, perfect body touted as ideal by our society. Some take their dissatisfaction in stride, but for others a perceived "imperfect" body is the source of psychological problems that cause them difficulties which can include an exercise addiction.

Is your exercise addiction rooted in a poor body image? Take this quiz and find out.

	YES	NO
1. Do you often think about your weight and wish you looked more "ideal"?	___	___
2. Do you find yourself envying people		

who have "perfect" legs, waist size, or
height?   ____ ____

3. Do you frequently try diets or exercise
   plans that promise to change a specific
   body area?   ____ ____

4. Do you think others will find you more
   attractive and likable if you lose weight
   and/or gain muscle?   ____ ____

5. Do you buy clothing only if it
   enhances a favorable aspect of your
   body?   ____ ____

6. When you think about the body
   characteristic that you are unhappy
   about (top-heavy, thigh-heavy, and so
   on) does it put you in a bad mood?   ____ ____

7. Do you feel a weight gain or loss of
   five pounds would change how you
   and others feel about you?   ____ ____

A yes answer to any of these questions indicates a poor
body image. Obviously, the more often you have checked off
a yes response, the more likely it is that body image is at the
base of your exercise addiction.

NORMAL DEVELOPMENT OF BODY IMAGE

All people, males and females, have feelings about themselves based on what they believe they're supposed to look
like, as well as what they *do* look like. This mental picture of
how one looks is called the body image. The normal development of body image begins in infancy as children learn to
differentiate between self and nonself. Newborns have no
concept that there are other people in the world; the warmth

of a mother's body and the satisfaction of warm milk are experienced as extensions of self. Early on they begin to distinguish between self and the outside, and then, during the first year, children begin to see themselves as unique and separate bodies distinct from others. They look in a mirror and learn to recognize themselves. They put their own thumb in their mouth and recognize it as a part of themselves; thus begins the process of body-image development.

DISTORTION OF BODY IMAGE

The process of body-image development continues throughout one's lifetime and is influenced, positively and negatively, by many factors. Unfortunately there are a host of negative influences that can cause people to grow up with a distorted body image. The first and most influential comes from exposure to parental attitudes about their own bodies. If a parent is always dieting, complaining about his or her own body, or in any other way demonstrating excessive concern about weight and body shape, a child learns that a perfect body, or the quest for one, is a valued goal. Or if a parent flexes power by forcing a child to eat certain foods in a certain way (often with the good intention of ensuring nourishment), that child may learn that food can be used to control others.

During the teen years, peers and the media join with parental attitudes to influence an adolescent's body image. Because the onset of puberty varies, occurring for some at age ten or eleven and much later for others at age fifteen or sixteen, teenagers can suffer through several years of peer comparisons that make them feel "too tall," "too short," "too flat-chested," "too big," "too skinny," "too fat," and "too" anything else that a body can be. A positive body image easily gets lost in these years of trying to fill the gap between what one looks like and what one *wants* to look like.

It's especially difficult for girls to develop an acceptable body image. As their bodies change and they develop hips and breasts, they are not quite far enough along in the maturation process to be womanly, nor can they remain childlike. Also, every girl approaches puberty with her own ideas and feelings about what it means to become a woman. Parental comments like "You've got to eat more if you ever want to get rid of those skinny legs," or "Keep eating like that and we'll have to roll you out the door and down to school" plant the seeds of distortion into the developing body images of these girls.

Extreme body-image distortion probably leads some girls to suffer the eating problems of anorexia or bulimia nervosa. A full discussion of these disorders as direct causes of exercise addiction can be found in chapter 6.

Girls are additionally (and at times exceptionally) influenced in their body-image development by their fathers. As a young girl's sexuality is unfolding, her ideas about what is desirable and undesirable to the opposite sex will often come from her father. Off-the-cuff remarks may therefore be taken as the carved-in-stone opinions of all males. A father who prefers full-bodied women, for example, may kid his slim teen about her "tomboy" body. Or a father who likes svelte women may in good humor warn his plump daughter about the lonely life of chubby women. Careless comments like these may have long-standing effects.

At times, a girl who has problems with her mother may admire and identify with her father. She may reject the changes in her body because they make her look more like her mother and strive in many ways (perhaps intellectually and emotionally) to pattern herself after her father. She may even try to hide her growing femininity in an effort to look less like her mother and more like her father. Many subtle interactions between mother and daughter and daughter and father can unintentionally, yet easily, distort a young girl's body image.

These family problems compound the problems of body-image development because it is during puberty that many girls first begin to look for self-worth in their bodies; not finding it, they begin dieting. They diet with friends; they experiment with fasting and other faddish diets; and they mimic the diets of their favorite video stars. They stop and start these diets over and over again. By the ages of eighteen to twenty many have experienced their bodies in a number of different ways—from very thin to normal weight to slightly or even considerably overweight. Because of these constant variations in size, they now have no recognition or identification of a particular body size.

Adolescence is a time for individuation, separation from family, and the development of an adult self. Late adolescence is a time of consolidation of identity, but if there is an ever-changing physical appearance, no stable identification with a physical self develops. When this happens, these young women remain highly susceptible to external pressures, and, in conjunction with other risk factors, eating and exercise disorders emerge.

In adulthood, body image continues to be influenced by peers and media, but now the effects of narcissistic personality traits also come into play. Classic narcissists see themselves as perfect. In general, they feel they are more beautiful, more worthy, and entitled to more than anyone else. Although this grandiose view of self may create problems, it is actually the "reverse narcissists" who have body-image problems that are most readily driven to exercise addiction. Reverse narcissists hate themselves because they do not match up to the grandiose goals they set for themselves, body image being a prime example. These people strive to be perfect and can't accept themselves until they are. To many (particularly women in our culture), perfectionism and thinness are irrevocably linked and they cannot accept themselves as "worthy" until they have the perfect body. Their drive for perfection and thinness becomes one and the same; to be perfect, one must be thin, and if one isn't thin, one is seriously flawed. Reverse narcissists often use a concrete schedule of exercise to give them the comforting feeling of "I can reach perfection if I just keep trying." For psychological reasons, they can't rely on their own feelings and observations, so they need tangible activity to affirm their specialness. A rigid schedule allays the anxiety of imperfection by providing a structure with which to reach perfection.

MEN AND WOMEN AND THEIR BODY IMAGES

Men, as a group, are often much more satisfied with their bodies than are women. Body image may be more stable in men because our culture conveys the message that it is not important for a man to possess a perfect body to attain a position of power or to be admired and loved. Fat men (generally called stocky) who reach an influential and lucrative career status will be admired for what they have achieved rather than for how they look. However, it has been observed by today's sociologists that women who proceed through the ranks of the powerful and who possess a socially acceptable or desirable body size are often treated very differently from heavier and thus less socially approved women. When perfect-bodied women do arrive at an enviable position, it is often suggested that looks rather than brains brought them success.

The adage "You can never be too rich or too thin" seems especially ingrained in women who believe that body size, personal attractiveness, and self-worth are related. For those women who believe that they are more likely to be loved and to find a husband if they have the "right" body size, the problems of poor body image can have far-reaching negative effects. A perspective on the social politics of body image is fully discussed in Susie Orbach's book *Fat Is a Feminist Issue*. In the context of this chapter it's notable that in the general population women are prone to exercise addictions and other psychological problems rooted in poor body image because they are much more likely than men to be exceptionally body conscious.

In the world of athletics, however, the numbers of males and females with body-image problems begin to balance out. In 1987, *Runner's World* magazine sponsored the "Runner's Survey on Dieting and Eating."[1] This survey found that a surprisingly high number of both low- and high-mileage runners have a high degree of concern about body weight and dieting. In response to the question "Do you consciously watch your weight?" 73 percent of the females and 63 percent of the males answered "often" or "always." When asked "How satisfied are you with your current body size and shape?" 57 percent of the females and 37 percent of the males said "moderately satisfied" or worse. Apparently, even well-trained athletes who have no visible body-size or -shape problems can fall victim to body-image distortions. This information supports the finding that people who are merely five pounds overweight are often more concerned about losing weight than people who are obese, and therefore too far from perfection to be overly concerned about it. In our culture the advertising industry has convinced near-normal-weight people that "perfect" thinness is tied closely to success, happiness, and personal worth, and so the need to exercise excessively to gain perfection is fostered socially. The correlation between self-worth and perceived body size seems to be a complex psychological problem for many physically fit individuals.

When distorted body image and attempts to normalize it take psychological precedence over most other important life issues, the problem of size perception becomes patholog-ical. Again, among runners who look as if they could eat, drink, and not worry, the responses regarding body-size obsession were striking. Based on the number of respon-dents who answered "often," "usually," or "always" to given statements, 48 percent of the females and 21 percent of the males said they are "terrified" about the possibility of being overweight. Thirty-five percent of the females and 16 percent of the males find themselves preoccupied with thoughts of food, while 20 percent of the females and 7 percent of the males feel extremely guilty after eating, and a whopping 48 percent of the females and 24 percent of the males are preoccupied with a desire to be thinner. The fact that runners are among the people most likely to be in good to excellent physical condition highlights the irrational and unrealistic nature of their body-image concerns.

It is this irrational concern with body size and shape that leads untold numbers of people into excessive exercise in an effort to attain the perfect, or what they see as merely "ac-ceptable," body.

THE ADDICTION

People who suffer from intensely distorted body images look for ways to transform themselves into new and better individuals. Some try extreme diets; others seek plastic surgery or liposuction, and many spend vacation time at expensive "health" resorts. At some point in their search, most try exercise—some get hooked.

At first, exercise gives results that are fast and impressive. A dedicated exerciser can knock off several pounds and inches in the first few weeks. This initial fix bolsters exercisers' hopes of attaining and maintaining their fantasy image. This psychological lift helps them stick to their strict exercise regime even when they're tired, busy, or ill. As the body builds up tolerance to the quick expenditure of calories, the metabolism slows down and the obvious results are reduced. Now, to obtain the same level of benefits, exercisers need to increase the frequency, intensity, and duration of their workouts. This leads to a frustrating cycle of increased intensity reaping decreased benefits. And thus begins their addiction. Once a rigid routine is established over a period of time, exercisers find that they begin to crave their workouts. Exercise becomes a concrete action in their attempt to possess a slim body. As long as they are exercising, they can convince themselves that there is a possibility that the goal will be met.

An exercise addiction with roots in a poor body image can be maintained by a lack of understanding about how body size, diet, and exercise are related. Far too many exercisers base desirability of body size solely on the numbers on a bathroom scale. Debbie was determined to drop 10 pounds from her base of 135. She began to work out at the gym on Nautilus and free weights three days a week and to run on weekends. At the same time, she joined a weight-control program for which she followed a prescribed diet plan and weighed in once a week. In eight weeks time, Debbie had dropped two clothing sizes. Rather than celebrating her "new" body, however, Debbie was upset and disappointed because although her physical size and appearance had improved, her weight had *increased* by 5 pounds; therefore she felt she had not met her original goal. To add to her misery, the weight-control program had a policy of fining participants who did not lose weight; thus, although inches had disappeared, Debbie was fined. Because Debbie didn't understand that when muscles are strengthened and toned, leaner is not necessarily lighter, she doubled her exercise efforts. Although she had been cautioned against lifting weights more than every other day, she began to lift every day and run every night in the misguided, and now dangerous, belief that the reading on the bathroom scale was the only "real" way to judge the shape of her body. Once hooked into this rigid routine, Debbie was showing signs of addiction. Now she continues to work out every day in her drive to lose weight even though her physical size more than meets her original mental image.

Thirty-six-year-old Rosemary is also addicted to exercise because of her unrealistic evaluation of her appearance. Rosemary had watched men stare at the tall, thin girls with long shapely legs. She promised herself that someday soon she would be the object of similar interest. She began a vigorous exercise routine, canceling social appointments more and more frequently, and turning down invitations that interfered with her exercise schedule before and after work. She also began a strict diet that she stuck to in the same rigid and uncompromising fashion. Rosemary was determined not to let anything keep her from reaching her goal. After three months, Rosemary had lost nine pounds, but she still felt she was not "thin" and her legs were not "shapely"—and so she continued her exercise and diet routine. After two more months, she had lost another four and a half pounds, but still had not met her goal. After six months of continued dieting and exercising, Rosemary's body was still not "thin," and her legs (especially the thighs) resembled what she called "tree trunks," even though her friends perceived a positive difference. But because she had not attained her image of tall, thin, and willowy, she bolstered her sense of determination, further reduced her daily caloric intake, and increased her exercise sessions. She did all of this without considering the luck of the genetic draw, which dictates that exercise and diet cannot always change body type and will never make an adult woman grow taller.

Heredity can dictate the way our bodies respond to food and exercise. Our bone size and density, the number of fat cells, and metabolic responses converge to create our actual body size and shape. When overweight, we can all reduce calories and lose excess pounds and use exercise to tone muscles, but diet and exercise cannot reshape our genetic structure. Still, thousands of people like Rosemary pursue an unattainable goal that causes them to stick to a rigid exercise schedule and suffer all of the negative characteristics of their addiction without ever having a chance of developing the body size they seek.

On the other hand, some people have the genetic propensity toward long and lean bodies but for various reasons see themselves as overweight. Ralph, for example, was twenty to thirty pounds overweight during his childhood and adolescence. During his college years, Ralph began a daily exercise program of weight lifting and playing basketball for fun and social interaction; coincidentally, he dropped the excess pounds and began to build healthy muscle mass and tone. Now, at age thirty-eight, Ralph continues to work out every day. Although it often interferes with job and family obligations, he can't allow himself a break because he still sees himself as overweight. He feels like the heavy and socially isolated adolescent that he was—although this brief period of being overweight was shorter than the twenty years of fitness that have intervened. Ralph is obsessed with shedding imaginary fat and in the process has become addicted to exercise. As he continues to exercise excessively and lose imaginary fat, his goal is clearly an unhealthy one.

Similar to the case of Ralph, some people, especially women, who have lost a lot of weight actually do "see" themselves as fat and so they continue on excessive exercise regimens. Quite commonly, it can take an extended period for these people to come to experience their bodies as small and fit—some never make this adjustment. This slow or nonexistent adjustment may be the result of a poor body image caused by psychological experiences in childhood or puberty. It is thought that perhaps the brain actually receives old signals that relay the fat body image long after the body size has physically changed. Whatever the cause, this distorted image pushes its victims into unnecessary and ultimately unhealthy exercise programs.

A poor body image can arise from many and varied sources. These distortions can later bring people to set body maintenance goals that, like Debbie's, are unnecessary or, like Rosemary's, are unattainable or, like Ralph's, are outdated. However, if the poor body image is addressed through an intense program of exercise and no attempts are made to understand its basis, it can lead to an addiction that interferes with physical and psychological well-being.

THE PROBLEM

Rejection of one's self is the antithesis of healthy exercise goals. In its intended and best form, exercise can improve and maintain body health and fitness as well as improve psychological functioning. Excessive exercise problems that are based in distorted body images have little to do with an effort to enhance physical well-being; in these cases, exercise is used as a mechanism to modify a problem with self-acceptance and self-worth.

A psychologically healthy view of exercise is one that says "I'm exercising to stay in shape, but I know that my body size, whether heavy or thin, doesn't dictate who I am or what kind of person I am." However, as an addict your view probably says "If only my abdomen were flat, people would like me. If only my thighs were thinner, I'd like myself. If only my body were smaller, I'd be happy." For those whose addiction is rooted in a poor body image, the exercise program does not stem only from a physical need to drop some weight; it grows from pathological attempts at self-improvement.

If you carefully analyze your attitudes about exercising, you'll find that you don't need to see any physical body changes to stay motivated and to continue your routine. You probably feel worthy and attractive, though never perfect, as long as you're engaged in the *effort* to achieve body perfection. The fact that you can muster the discipline and energy to strive for this goal creates a sense that you are in control and it establishes a new identity for you as an athlete— something you've probably come to admire. Many addicts depend on exercise for a positive self-image.

As mentioned earlier, narcissism involves an inordinate interest in one's self. Narcissistic exercisers are ones who already find themselves beautiful and enjoy the opportunity to show off their bodies at the gym and to watch themselves with great admiration. You may have seen men with very muscular bodies lifting weights at the gym. They place themselves in front of the mirror and watch their workout in complete self-absorption. Also, you know of women with near-perfect bodies and designer workout gear in aerobic classes who love each moment they watch their bodies move. These exercisers cannot separate who they are from the way they look; they must keep exercising to reinforce their belief that they are accomplished and worthwhile.

Less content, but equally determined to find a positive sense of self in exercise, are the reverse narcissists—those who hate themselves because they don't meet the grandiose goals they've set for themselves. One can easily imagine a woman or man who is a perfectionist in every aspect of life and who has been a lifelong overachiever. Although undoubtedly in good aerobic shape, and in great overall shape in the eyes of family and friends, this exerciser pushes beyond the limits of normal endurance to achieve not a good body but a great body, or to run not a very fast race but a race time to be expected of someone who devotes most of the day to running and training. Reverse narcissists never reach their goals of finding personal perfection in exercise, and so their addiction continues unabated.

This dependence on exercise for self-worth and positive body image sets up the dangers inherent in withdrawal. What happens if you can't exercise because of business trips, family obligations, or illness? If your addiction is based in a poor body image, you lose all sense of self-worth and attractiveness. Suddenly, although your clothes still fit and there's no discernible change in your size, you're filled with self-loathing because you feel fat, ugly, and undesirable. A loss of a day's exercise, no matter how intense the routine, will never have a truly discernible effect on anything. Unfortunately, addicts can't believe this and all too often make important decisions that affect their ability to enjoy life based on this ill-perceived body image.

Ralph, for example, has decided to turn down job promotions that would require him to travel and possibly forfeit some of his workout time. He tells himself that he'll have a more promising career if he loses more weight. It does not occur to him that he has reduced his career status in order to exercise. He focuses single-mindedly on exercise as a means of self-perfection. Debbie, who began dieting and lifting weights to drop ten pounds for health reasons, is now worried that in a day without lifting all her muscles will turn into fat. She can't even give herself a break long enough to go with her family on vacation, or to be in charge of refreshments for her son's little league team. Without consciously deciding to ignore her family, Debbie is forced by her addiction to do so in her pursuit of a "trim" body.

Rosemary, too, who will never be tall and willowy, has actually canceled or rescheduled important business presentations when she knows she will be unable to exercise the night before. She fears that a room full of people will think she is as fat as she feels she is and therefore will assume she has no self-control. She, like Ralph and Debbie, doesn't realize that missing one day, or even two, of exercise will have *no* visible effect and that her attitudes are not rational. Rosemary has also sabotaged her original goal of meeting men by declining dates that interfere with her exercise schedule and by canceling those that are planned for days on which she can't exercise or after a day when she was forced to miss an aerobic workout. At the last business convention, Rosemary worried that the rich foods she'd been eating went directly to her hips for all the world to see. She felt deeply ashamed of herself for breaking her diet and for not exercising and so she hid in her room and skipped important meetings when she thought someone she knew might be there. Without an aerobic workout and without her running shoes, Rosemary became a nonfunctioning person.

THE REMEDY

Body image depends ultimately on what you *believe* is true about your body. The first step in changing painful and problematic thoughts is to identify them and determine what they really mean. This is rarely easy to do, however, because people with body-image distortions most often think they view themselves objectively. They don't recognize that there is a problem in how they *think* about their bodies. Some size-five, 110-pound women, for example, believe they have "gargantuan" thighs. These women have two problems: first, in their need to focus so intently on their thighs; second, in their inclination to distort what they see. Clearly, this is distorted perception.

To elicit your personal body image, ask yourself some questions that highlight negative perceptions. For example, how would you feel about yourself if you just ate a double hot fudge sundae? What is your reaction when someone remarks that you look as if you've gained some weight? How do you feel when you're standing next to someone with a "perfect" body?

After identifying thoughts such as "I feel fat," or "I'm overweight," or "I'm all flab," or "I'm too short," you need to examine how rational these thoughts are. Have you actually gained weight or are you just frightened you will? Do the comments of others on your appearance trigger inner feelings of dissatisfaction and shame? Do the negative feelings about your body become especially acute at certain times, such as after you've eaten a "forbidden" food, after an unsuccessful sports competition, when you're lonely, or when you are angry with yourself about work or something else? To determine the reality of your body image, you should imagine how a friend might react if you were to confess just how upset you feel. Would your friend say, "Yes, missing one workout definitely caused you to gain at least three pounds and now you look obese."

You can also become closer attuned to reality by looking at how you judge others relative to how you judge yourself. Is your friend, who is the same clothing size as you, as repulsive to you as you feel to yourself? Or are you using different standards to assess yourself and others? Do your friends suddenly look obese to you when their busy work schedules keep them from exercising for a day or even for a full week? Or are you the only one who goes from tolerable to obese after a day or two of no exercise?

When you experience negative body-image feelings, try to give yourself some kind of objective confirmation of these feelings. Weigh yourself at the time you feel "fat." Remind yourself that everyone's weight goes up and down by a few pounds even during the course of one day. Ask a trusted friend if you really have gargantuan thighs or a flabby stomach. Also, try to identify the intangible beliefs and values that go along with your feelings. Grab hold of the following kinds of thoughts and hold them up to examination.

• I want to be thin because people who are thin are always successful, happy, and attractive.

• I want to be thin because it indicates that I have the discipline to control my appetite and my exercising.

• I'm weak and self-indulgent because I ate a cookie and didn't work out today.

• One deviation from my workout schedule makes me a total failure.

• Fat people are out of control and self-indulgent; so am I when I miss a part of my exercise schedule.

To remedy an exercise addiction rooted in these kinds of thoughts, your attitudes about happiness, success, self-indulgence, and self-worth need to be separated from feelings about the body. Push yourself to set aside your imagined "ideal" body and come to terms with your "real" body. Are you, for example, a six-foot two-inch large-boned man who, because you want to run like Salazar, is upset by your height, breadth, weight, and anything else that is not pure lean muscle? Or, perhaps you are a five-foot two-inch woman who has always admired the tall magazine models. Do you hate yourself for your physical "flaws" and believe you should somehow be able to create a model image if not the actuality? Or are you a five-foot eight-inch wiry man who adores football stars? It may be time to unburden yourself and admit that some fantasies are unattainable and can be destructive. You need to focus on your own physical characteristics and find a new role model to represent another idea of the ideal.

Some severe body-image distortion problems need to be confronted vigorously. Are you purposely avoiding your body? Do you stay away from mirrors? Dress or undress in the dark? Refuse to look down while showering? If you do these things, you need to confront what is and isn't distorted in the way you view yourself. To do this, try these easily implemented ideas.

• Look at yourself in the mirror for five minutes. Try to push out all judgmental thoughts; just look.

• Stop wearing shapeless clothes that have no waistline. You may think you're hiding, but you lose the contours of your body and can more easily imagine it in distorted ways.

• Go to exercise classes wearing a leotard and watch yourself work out.

- Watch your muscles.
- If you have access to a video camera, make a tape of yourself wearing the outfits you think hide your despised body part or quality. Then add a segment of yourself in clothes that you think "reveal" this awful body. Look at the tape as though you were seeing some other person and try to decide honestly if that loathsome quality is really as visible as you feel it is.

If you can identify your problem thoughts and honestly determine if they reflect reality, you'll find that your need to exercise excessively will also be exposed by the light of reality. This awareness, combined with the facts about exactly what exercise can and cannot do to change your body type (as detailed in chapters 7 and 8) will help you create a healthy, nonaddictive exercise program.

If none of the approaches in this chapter help you to recognize the need to change your perceptions rather than your body size, you may need to seek professional help. Group therapy is usually the most successful in this area. This is especially so in groups comprised of people who share similar problems and which are led by a therapist skilled specifically in the cognitive group techniques that have proved valuable in working with body-image problems. Group therapy provides a reality test. You hear what others say about your body and you hear what they think about their own. The others may challenge your feelings about yourself, and you, too, will see how others whom you deem attractive and fit can feel that they are obese or too fat in the thighs, hips, buttocks, or stomach area.

6

Eating Disorder Exercisers

If I eat this cookie, I'll have to exercise an extra half hour tonight to work off the calories; on the other hand, if I exercise for an extra hour, I can have two cookies.

A typical case of exercise addiction based on an eating disorder is found in twenty-eight-year-old Kathleen of New York City who is an attractive, successful, and high-powered career woman. At five each morning the alarm jars her from sleep and in the rote steps of her daily routine she heads for the running path in Central Park. After completing her five-mile run, Kathleen returns home for a quick shower, a gulp of coffee, and then she's back out battling through midtown traffic.

Kathleen likes to be in complete control of her life. She arrives at the office by 8:30 every morning and uses her perfectionist drive and superior intellect to keep ahead of the other young lawyers grappling for a promotion in one of the city's most prestigious law firms. Kathleen doesn't mind working through lunch. In fact, because she's watching her weight, Kathleen would rather eat a quick salad at her desk than take time to eat a full meal. Suppers are also swallowed on the go because when she leaves work at seven o'clock each night Kathleen heads to the gym for an hour of aerobics and a one-mile swim. Then it's home to bed before eleven o'clock so she can get enough rest before her morning run.

From a distance, it looks like Kathleen has it all—she is a successful lawyer and an attractive, slim woman. But a closer look reveals a well-kept secret that if left unchecked may interfere with her carefully planned climb to the top. Like millions of other women (and an increasing number of men), Kathleen has an eating disorder. Her desperate need for total control over her body size and shape has pushed her into abnormal eating patterns and she has recently coupled that problem with an addiction to exercise. Because exercise is socially admired, Kathleen has found that she can easily use it to support her eating disorder and at the same time mask the problem from herself and others.

Are you using exercise to maintain abnormal eating habits? Take this quiz to find out.

	YES	NO
1. Do you find that you regularly adjust your exercise according to how much you ate earlier or on the preceding day?	___	___
2. Are you concerned to terrified about being overweight?	___	___
3. Did your interest in exercise begin with a desire to lose weight?	___	___
4. Do you fear not exercising each day because you think you'll gain weight?	___	___
5. Are you preoccupied with food and calories and calculate what you are "allowed" to eat each day according to how much time you can give to exercise?	___	___

6. Have you gone on eating binges
   where you feel you cannot stop?   ____ ____
7. Do you exercise an excessive amount
   after a binge (both *excessive amount*
   and *binge* being self-defined as much
   more than usual for you)?   ____ ____
8. Are you preoccupied with being
   thinner, having a low body mass/lean
   muscle ratio—as elite athletes often
   do?   ____ ____
9. Do you think about burning calories
   as you exercise?   ____ ____
10. Do you ever vomit, take laxatives or
    diuretics after a meal or a binge to
    feel thinner or to lose the calories?   ____ ____
11. Do you feel virtuous when dieting,
    restricting your dietary intake, or
    exercising?   ____ ____
12. Do others tell you that you're too thin
    or exercise too much?   ____ ____

If you find that you answer yes to six or more of these questions, your exercise addiction may be based in an eating disorder.

Eating disorders and excessive exercise go hand in hand for many of the country's finest athletes. A recent study of female athletes at Michigan State University found that 74 percent of gymnasts, 45 percent of long-distance runners, 50 percent of field-hockey players, and 25 percent of varsity softball players, volleyball players, tennis players, and track runners use abnormal dieting methods.[1] In 1987 *American-Statesman* reported that one out of every ten female athletes at the University of Texas had been diagnosed as having a serious eating disorder. Among these were 1984 double gold medalist Tiffany Cohen, who had to be hospitalized for nine weeks in 1988 for her eating disorder, and 1984 Olympic breaststroker Kim Rhodenbaugh, who underwent six months of outpatient treatment for a similar problem.[2] Also notable on the list of athletes with a history of eating disorders are Olympic gymnast Cathy Rigby and exercise enthusiast Jane Fonda. The deadly combination of diet and exercise is additionally illustrated in two current books: dancer Gelsey Kirkland's *Dancing on My Grave* (Doubleday) and distance-runner Mary Wazeter's *Dark Marathon* (Zondervan Books). Ironically, for all of these exercisers it was the need to gain total control over their bodies that wrenched that control from their grip and left them further out of control.

Eating disorders are generally labeled as one of two types: anorexia nervosa or bulimia nervosa. Each has distinct characteristics that will be discussed separately, but because each can combine with exercise to threaten an individual's physical and psychological well-being, the problems caused by an exercise addiction with its roots in eating disorders will be discussed jointly.

ANOREXIA NERVOSA

Anorexia nervosa is an eating disorder characterized by self-imposed starvation. Although this problem has received ample media attention only in the last fifteen to twenty years, the illness is not new. It was described in the medical literature of England and France over a hundred years ago and was named by a physician of that time, Sir William Gull. Of course, a lot has been learned about this disorder since that time. We now know that a victim does not refuse to eat because of a "lack of appetite" (which is what the word *anorexia* means) but rather because of complex psycho-sociological factors that drive her to exert strict self-control by denying herself food.

Today, the *Diagnostic and Statistical Manual of Mental Disorders* (3d rev. ed.) sets forth these four criteria for the diagnosis of anorexia nervosa:

1. The fear of being fat even when at or below normal weight
2. Refusal to maintain body weight by restricting intake, leading to a weight loss of more than 15 percent of normal body weight
3. A distortion of body size and shape that causes even underweight sufferers to feel fat or obese
4. In women, the absence of at least three consecutive menstrual cycles, reflecting amenorrhea

Anyone who meets these four criteria is clearly anorectic. But there are also millions who, although starving themselves, do not meet these standards of formal diagnosis. For the purposes of this book, the label of anorectic will be applied to the eating disorders experienced by those who meet the above criteria, as well as to the eating problems of those whose severe restriction of food has become the focus of their lives.

Ninety-five percent of anorectics are females who generally experience the onset of symptoms between the ages of twelve and twenty-five. They are often the firstborn children of socioeconomically advantaged families and grow up in an environment that rewards education and achievement. These girls do well in school and are portraits of perfect daughters who, before the onset of their eating disorder, were touted by proud parents as ideal children. The problem often starts when a teenage girl decides, or is even advised by a doctor, to "lose a little weight." As she begins to lose, the weight loss itself becomes gratifying.

Food gives these girls and women an arena where they can exert their own form of control. Their thin bodies become their pride and joy and serve as concrete evidence of their willpower and self-discipline. They are obsessed with counting calories and often weigh themselves several times a day. Many create elaborate eating rituals, such as slowly, carefully, and meticulously organizing food on a plate, or dawdling over food and methodically chewing each small piece a specified number of times, or cutting the food into extremely small pieces. As pounds drop off, thoughts of food and how to avoid it become the central preoccupation of the anorectic's day. Moreover, the less they eat over time, the less acutely they feel the physical sensation of hunger, giving them feelings of power and control.

Anorectics have distorted body images that cause them to see themselves as being much larger than they really are. When asked to look at themselves in the mirror and draw a picture of what they see they will typically draw a figure three times their actual body size. There is speculation in the research community that this perceptual distortion may be caused by the same phantom-limb phenomenon that gives the sensation of arms and legs to amputees. Tissue lost through starvation diets may have continuing representation in the body image. This hallucinatory perception is a consistent variable in this disorder and may be caused by interruption in the afferent nerves that go to the brain from the body. This change in the nervous system may cause anorectics not to see the diminishing change in their body size. (See chapter 5 for a fuller discussion of body-image problems.)

Theories regarding the causes of anorexia nervosa are

varied and controversial. Because anorexia nervosa often appears in thirteen- and fourteen-year-old girls, it seems that, in part, it may be a psychological disturbance related to the process of growing up and becoming a woman. By severely restricting food intake, it is possible to keep hips and breasts from maturing and to stop or delay the onset of menstruation. It may also be a form of adolescent rebellion or a way of calling attention to substantial concerns with self-image. For other sufferers the onset of anorexia nervosa commonly coincides with a girl's entrance into college. A girl who fears this step into adulthood and the opportunity for sexual relationships may unconsciously strive to stop the maturation process through self-starvation. This often takes a developed eighteen-year-old back to her twelve-year-old body. It is also probable that many anorectics have learned from the movies, TV, and advertising to equate being loved and respected with being thin. Almost all anorectics have a need to be admired and loved, but feeling unworthy of such attention, they seek drastic measures to become perfect and therefore worthy. Paradoxically, this behavior ensures feedback from family and friends but only out of concern for the anorectic's health. It is the anorectic who sees beauty and perfection; others see an emaciated body.

In typical cases these women eventually suffer the physical consequences of malnutrition: skeletonlike appearance, anemia, dry skin, soft and fine body hair growth (called lanugo), low body temperature, and a lowered metabolism. The psychological mind-set that forces them into this preoccupation with food and body size is often accompanied by social withdrawal and the intense need to control their appetites. Concentrating on controlling food helps them repress less obvious but problematic states, all or most of which remain hidden from the anorectic's conscious thought.

THE ADDICTION

An estimated 150,000 American females suffer from anorexia nervosa. A rapidly increasing number use exercise to limit even further the number of calories available for fat production. This condition, sometimes referred to as anorexia athletica, increases the risk of physical harm and fosters the addictive quality of the eating disorder.

Young anorectics generally begin their efforts to lose weight solely by restricting food intake. They then discover their bodies' metabolism decreases the rate of calorie consumption to compensate for the reduction in food. That's often when they'll turn to exercise as an added calorie burner. The exercises of choice are usually those that can be practiced without great skill, without a partner, and without competition. The anorectic usually participates in a sport solely as a means of weight control; she's not interested in excelling at it. The anorectic is also aware that although she can push herself to exercise despite her weakened physical state, she would not be capable of sustained competition. She will therefore gravitate to exercise regimens that can be done alone and at one's own pace. These include running, aerobics, and calisthenics.

The preoccupation with exercise experienced by some anorectics often greatly resembles their obsessive interest in food and calories. Once an anorectic begins exercising she will do anything to fit it into her schedule. One young anorectic patient was hospitalized because she had lost so much weight she was in danger of starving to death. During her stay she was told to remain bedridden because she should not even expend the calories required to walk. This otherwise bright and accomplished girl was found doing sit-ups in her bed whenever she was left alone in her room.

People suffering anorexia athletica are truly addicted to exercise and, as this young girl illustrates, will do anything to stay in motion.

BULIMIA NERVOSA

Bulimia is an eating disorder characterized by a binge-purge syndrome. Bulimics have recurrent and uncontrollable episodes of binge eating in which they rapidly consume an inordinate amount of food. It would not be unusual for a bulimic to eat two dozen cupcakes, a quart of ice cream, three candy bars, and four hard rolls at one sitting. Appropriately, the word *bulimia* means "ox hunger." After an eating binge, the bulimic feels an equally urgent need to eliminate (purge) the gorged food through some self-induced method such as vomiting, enemas, starvation, laxatives, and/or diuretics. Recently exercise has been added to this list of purgative devices. Bulimics addicted to exercise try to eat only if they can exercise and exercise because they know they will binge soon again, or because they want to compensate for the last binge.

The *Diagnostic and Statistical Manual for Mental Disorders* (3d rev. ed.) lists these four criteria for the diagnosis of bulimia:

1. Recurrent episodes of binge eating (at least two times a week for at least three months)
2. A feeling of complete loss of control during the eating binges
3. Persistent overconcern with body shape and size
4. The person regularly engages in self-induced vomit-

ing, use of laxatives or diuretics, strict dieting or fasting, or vigorous exercise in order to prevent weight
gain.

Anyone who meets these four criteria is diagnosed as
suffering from bulimia nervosa. Others who may binge only
once a week or even once every two weeks are also considered bulimic for the purposes of our discussion because
they, too, feel equally out of control and seek drastic means
to compensate.

Often, bulimics are well-groomed, attractive, successful
women of normal weight who are very concerned with
physical perfection. This trait of perfectionism often pushes
them to strive for superior achievement professionally. Surprisingly, bulimics often suffer from low self-esteem and a
need for validation from others. When the reassurance from
others is not forthcoming, or something depresses them,
bulimics typically turn to food as a means of nurturing
themselves. These binges signal a loss of control and fill the
bulimic with guilt, self-loathing, and shame. Purging is then
used to "undo" the binge both physically and psychologically and as a renewed drive for perfection.

Unlike anorectics, bulimics are not solely limited to mid-
dle- and upper-class families with high expectations. Bulimia knows no class or income barrier. Also unlike
anorectics, bulimics do not stand out with a skeletonlike
appearance. Their weight is typically within the normal
range, and because the binge-purge cycles are performed in
secret, causing subtle physical changes, family and friends
often remain unaware of the problem.

Although some bulimics can hide their disorder and
maintain a normal (even admirable) physical appearance,
they are still in danger of experiencing starvation. Recent

research has shown many bulimics have a genetically low basal metabolic rate (BMR). A person's BMR determines how many calories are needed to maintain bodily functions while at complete rest. A person with a low BMR uses calories at a slower pace and so needs less food to gain weight than someone with a high BMR who uses calories rapidly and thus needs more food simply to maintain weight. According to recent research, it appears that some anorectics start out with a relatively high BMR and so when they cut their caloric intake, they can lose weight quite rapidly. But bulimics, with their low BMR, often eat very little between binges and purge after each binge, yet still do not lose weight. As in any starvation situation, the body reacts to the lack of food by lowering its metabolic rate to hold on to every calorie it possibly can. In the anorectic food restriction reduces the BMR to a lower level, but in the bulimic the level drops from its already low starting point to an even lower level. To stay at what appears to be a normal weight, bulimics may actually be starving themselves and risking acute malnutrition just as anorectics are in more obvious ways. Binges rarely make up for the purging or restricting because most often bulimics gravitate to high-calorie, high-carbohydrate, or high-fat foods that may not be nutritionally sound.

The causes of bulimia appear to overlap with other psychological and biological problems. It has recently been found that there may be a neurochemical predisposition to the development of bulimia. A study has documented that bulimics seem to have an abnormality in the satiety center located in the hypothalamus portion of their brains.[3] In this center, a neurotransmitter called serotonin tells people when they are full after eating. People of normal weight, as well as those who are obese, underweight, and even anorectic, all report having the feeling of satiety after eating.

Bulimics, however, feel hungrier as they eat. Their brains do not seem to readily transmit feelings of fullness, and consequently they have no biological cue that they have eaten adequately.

This same neurotransmitter is also involved in depression, and while it is not yet known how or if bulimia is neurochemically related to depression, it is known that bulimics are generally more depressed than others. Bulimics who choose exercise as their method of purging are less depressed than nonexercising bulimics. This use of exercise may be especially addictive because bulimics gravitate to exercise not only to purge the calories and to psychologically undo the guilt of an eating binge but also because it helps control their feelings of depression and anxiety.

Not uncommonly, bulimics exhibit obsessive-compulsive personality traits. In fact, bulimia and obsessive-compulsive disorder are probably both mediated through the brain's neurotransmitter serotonin. Obsessive-compulsive personalities (distinct from those with obsessive-compulsive disorder) seek complete control over their time schedule and environment. The bulimic, too, must be able to schedule time for binging and purging. When the purge method of choice for a bulimic with obsessive-compulsive traits is exercise, the stage is set for exercise addiction. In this situation, exercise is used to compensate for the caloric intake of a binge as well as to schedule a rigid routine that discharges the obsessive-compulsive anxiety caused by uncertainty and the loss of control.

Although the causes of bulimia are complex, elusive, and multifactorial, the victims all follow the same pattern of self-destructiveness. These women suffer from extreme body-image distortions. Although they often see themselves more realistically than do women with anorexia, they don't like to look in the mirror at all. If they do, they will show facial gestures of intense disgust that make clear feelings of "This body is awful; I hate the fact that it belongs to me." These feelings can push the binge-purge cycle into motion. (See chapter 5 for a more complete explanation of body-image distortions.)

Binge-purge cycles that rely on vomiting, laxatives, diuretics, or restrictive dieting can leave the bulimic with a host of medical problems that can include dehydration and dry skin, constipation from lack of body fluids, muscle spasm, kidney problems, and even cardiac arrest, which can be brought on by an electrolyte imbalance caused by loss of body fluids. Electrolyte imbalance, with its many serious complications, is an especially likely possibility if the bulimic combines one of these purgatives with exercise. Sweating further depletes the body's supply of electrolytes and minerals; when the body is already suffering an imbalance, the results can be extremely hazardous.

A common scenario of bulimia features a young, normal-weight, attractive woman with a history of binging on large quantities of high-calorie foods for five years. She has compensated for these binges with self-induced vomiting and occasional laxatives, but most often she uses excessive dieting and exercise. She binges one day and the next day does two times her normal amount of exercise and eats only raw vegetables. She might then go back to her normal routine of a five-mile run and one aerobic class per day, but she will maintain a very restrictive eating pattern, consuming a maximum of 700 calories a day. This restrictive eating over the next few days inevitably leads to the next binge, the next ten-mile run and back-to-back aerobic classes and the same severe dieting, always with the promise never to binge again.

THE ADDICTION

At least one to two in a hundred American college women suffer from bulimia, and certainly there are younger and older victims. Many are finding a socially acceptable method of purging in exercise—giving rise to the term *exercise bulimia*. Clinically, exercise bulimia is really bulimia nervosa in which exercise is the predominant purging strategy. To maintain their weight, they may exercise as often as three times a day, schedule their lives around their exercise times, and become extremely aggravated and anxious if something happens to interfere with their exercise plans.

Exercise bulimics may not know they have an eating disorder. They're not sticking their fingers down their throats to vomit, nor are they abusing laxatives or pills. They are unconsciously using a psychological defense called undoing. Exercise is viewed as a harmless way to undo the effects of an eating binge and to regain control of their bodies. Exercise also provides the psychological impact of ridding bulimics of the guilt they often feel after a binge.

Unlike anorectics, who exercise alone and in noncompetitive situations, some bulimics are attracted to sports in which they can train, compete, and excel. They tend to become very involved in their workouts and aim to achieve superior proficiency. The true exercise bulimic rarely mixes exercise with purgative methods other than dieting. These would leave the body too weak to perform at its best.

Jannette is a twenty-three-year-old medical technician who has only recently realized that her five-year obsession with exercise has actually been due to an eating disorder. "I started running with friends in college as a way to lose weight. Although my clothing size hadn't changed, I had been feeling overweight since I was about seventeen. At that time, I started crazy eating habits; I'd eat a whole box of cookies late at night when everyone else was sleeping. Then I'd go back to normal eating for about a week. But then I'd lose control again and eat until I felt sick. When my friends in the dorm started jogging, I decided to go with them, hoping I'd lose some weight. I began running two miles, but soon advanced to five miles a day. Then I added aerobic classes three times a week to my schedule. Anytime I would eat more than a salad, I would count the calories and feel guilty. Since then every morsel of food I eat is calculated according to its calories and the amount of running or aerobics I'll need to perform to work it off. It has taken on a pattern where I usually starve myself for a few days, then break down in ravenous hunger and eat everything in sight. After each binge I torture myself with hours of grueling workouts. I feel I have to exercise even if it means running in awful weather, when I'm sick or injured, or even if I have to miss important appointments to do it. Everything comes second to getting rid of calories through exercise."

THE PROBLEM

Exercise addiction doesn't cause eating disorders; it compounds and complicates them. Because it's easy to pass off strenuous workouts as "healthy" and "good," it's also easy to use them as cover-ups for destructive starvation and/or binge-purge diets. Some anorectics push themselves through grueling exercise routines not only to expend calories but also to prove to themselves that their bodies are still strong and that they are not destroying themselves as their family and friends warn. The bulimic does the same after a binge, but she does it to prove that she is still in control of herself and to offset the guilt and self-directed anger her gorging causes. For these people, exercise serves as a smoke screen that interferes with their ability to recognize the destructive power of eating disorders.

Exercise addiction also adds a complex factor to the eating-disorder dilemma in that it is an addiction with all the inherent characteristics explained in chapter 1. Tolerance often sabotages the exercise goal of the anorectic and bulimic. The primary goal of an exercise addict with an eating disorder is to get rid of calories and fat. However, as a constant increase in exercise causes the body to build up tolerance, it becomes more difficult to work off the desired calories. This tolerance factor can be very frustrating to the anorectic or bulimic who could previously count on exercise to knock off excess pounds; after a while it takes more and more exercise to reach the same goal. Two hours at the gym must soon be stretched to three; a five-mile daily run isn't enough so three more miles are added on. The more time one puts into exercise, the more entrenched the addiction becomes.

Once exercise addiction has taken hold, exercise cravings strike more and more frequently, driving the anorectic or bulimic to exercise even when her eating problem has left her feeling weak or ill. It also interferes with her capacity to be involved with other people and activities. When each morsel consumed must be atoned for with time-consuming exercise regimens, there is often little time left for social engagements, family affairs, or business appointments. This drives a deeper wedge between the person with the eating disorder and those who might be able to help her battle the problem.

Anorectics and bulimics who use exercise in their weight-management system become physically and psychologically dependent upon it. Just as they need to be thin, they need to exercise. It is the same kind of dependence that enables drug addicts and alcoholics to function only if they obtain a daily fix. If something, such as an ankle sprain or business meeting, should interfere with scheduled exercise time, people with eating disorders become anxious, irritable, and depressed. If exercise time is denied on a long-term basis (because of an exercise-related injury, for instance), the frail psychological condition that led to the eating disorder will further weaken them and they may find that their depression will cause a severe recurrence of the eating-disorder symptoms. The feelings of depression may then become so intense that, for some, even suicide may be considered as a means of relief. It's also common, when an exercise bulimic can't exercise, to see an increase in binging and a substitution of another purging method such as self-induced vomiting or laxative abuse.

An eating disorder plus an exercise addiction has the potential to be extremely dangerous. Unfortunately, the combination is becoming increasingly common. In an effort to find how frequently eating-disordered behaviors appeared among a random sampling of runners, 200 questionnaires were distributed at four New York Road Runner's Club races. From the 180 responses, a surprisingly high number of runners were found to be caught up in the eat-to-run connection. In fact, 19 percent of the female runners were bulimic. A common source of runners' concern, among both sexes and at all levels of proficiency, was about how lost workouts would affect weight. Restrictive eating patterns developed as this concern grew, and with increasingly restrictive eating, one sees increasing frequency in binging. The relationship between eating and exercise is much more intricately intertwined than first suspected.[4]

THE REMEDY

A remedy for an eating disorder complicated by dependence on exercise is different from one for an eating disorder alone. In part, this is because people who are exercising increase their caloric needs, thereby compounding the danger of restrictive diets and purging. It's also true that because exercise is a socially admired activity that gives individuals with eating problems a sense of discipline, control, and positive recognition, it is doubly difficult to restructure their exercise *and* personal eating habits at the same time. For these reasons exercise-related eating disorders often require professional intervention as detailed later in this chapter. But self-help programs, such as the following remedies, might be tried in a gradual manner and in incremental steps to build normalized eating patterns while cutting down on exercise abuse. They may also be combined with the suggestions in chapter 7 that discuss generalized body-image problems.

EXERCISE BULIMIA

Three Meals a Day. Both athletic men and women tend to restrict their dietary intake in an effort to improve their body size, increase lean body mass, and improve their physical performance. Although a common practice, numerous studies have shown that extreme dietary restriction sets the stage for binging—both in the full syndrome of bulimia and in the occasional, nonclinical, I-just-couldn't-stop-eating type. As explained earlier in this chapter, people often try to undo the physical and emotional consequences of these binges with exercise and renewed restrictive dieting. The more they exercise and restrict, the hungrier they'll become, the more deprived they'll feel due to the restricting, and the more likely they are to binge again.

To the outsider this eating and exercising problem may seem easy to remedy. It's apparent that if these affected people would eat three well-balanced (but reasonably low-calorie) meals a day, they would not be as physically tempted to binge or to restrict, as guilt-ridden about their eating, or as much in need of an exercise purge. This self-imposed and yet normalized eating schedule would also give them a sense of control over their eating habits and lives so they wouldn't need to exercise to excess to prove to themselves or others that they can exert self-control. In time, they would also see that their weight remained steady or even dropped by eating three meals a day as opposed to constantly dieting and episodically losing control.

Although true, this of course is much easier said than done. Many people require structured and supportive programs to break the starve-binge-exercise cycle. Others can overcome their eating disorders with self-help programs, like the one outlined in this chapter, that follow a gradual, step-by-step process.

When you are used to eating a highly restrictive diet of perhaps only one meal a day, eating three meals and snacks each day is a difficult (and sometimes frightening) concept to adjust to—but that's what this remedy is all about. Before you try this approach, you can increase the likelihood of success by planning ahead. Write down one day's menu of three meals and two snacks. Decide exactly what foods you will eat and make sure those foods are readily available to you. The meals should be planned to include a reasonable amount of calories, so a piece of hard candy is not considered a meal. Your caloric intake should be based on your weight, energy expenditure, and individual needs. (References for nutritional plans for athletes can be found in Appendix A.)

There are two approaches that might make these suggestions easier:

1. Plan a three-meal-a-day diet even if you are not yet ready to implement it. This may help desensitize you to the *idea* of eating a balanced diet.

2. Make your three meals a lower calorie content than might be advisable given your level of activity, size, and weight. This may offset your worry that eating three meals each day will lead to weight gain. Once the three meals a day and snacks become less tinged with anxiety, you can add the carbohydrate, protein, or fat content needed to make your eating plan nutritionally sound.

When you've decided what you will eat, write down the time of day you'll eat it. You shouldn't let more than three hours lapse between eating a meal or snack. When you begin this three-meals-a-day diet, eating these meals and snacks at the times you plan should take precedence over all other activities. Even if you have to stop in the middle of a project to eat your planned apple—do it. This food break is vital to the success of your diet because once five or more hours have elapsed between eating periods, you've potentially set yourself up for a bout of overeating. You must also follow your written plan even if you want to eat before a scheduled eating time. By telling yourself "I can eat my apple in forty-five minutes," you may find it easier to resist the doughnut that's offered at the business meeting. This ability to resist, knowing a planned snack will occur shortly, is especially important in your efforts to stop spontaneous and uncontrollable eating because it's the unplanned snack that can set off the counterregulatory phenomenon that says "I already blew it, so why not keep eating?"

You'll be better able to stick to this plan if you avoid doing other things while you eat. Think only about savoring the food. If you eat while reading, watching TV, or working, you'll taste the food less, enjoy it less, and crave it more. At the scheduled time, sit down, concentrate on your food, and eat it slowly.

If you stick to your preplanned daily menu, you'll find you can better control eating binges in the evening. This is when people who have withheld food all day most often slip in their resolve and eat far more than they want to. Your three meals and two snacks should be enough to keep you from feeling the ravenous need to eat at night. Use part of your evenings to plan a new menu for the following day.

When you first begin this three-meals-a-day approach, you may feel disappointed when you add up your caloric intake. The number of calories will probably be higher than the number consumed on your previous diet plan. But if you keep a running tally, you'll find that after four or five days of eating the regimented three meals and two snacks each day, your caloric intake is lower than it was on your former restrictive diet, which led to episodic overeating and binging. You'll need to give yourself at least a full week of normalized eating before you can fairly judge the success or failure of this diet.

If you find that your eating pattern is so seriously disturbed you cannot force yourself to eat three meals a day, try this approach in smaller steps. Pick a time of day when your activities and feelings are least disturbed. (For most people this is the morning.) At this time, plan to eat one desirable and "reasonable" meal (for example, a bowl of cereal, a bagel, or fruit). Do this every day at the same time until it becomes a routine and you feel comfortable eating the full meal. Then add another meal and, finally, the third. Do this over a time period you feel comfortable with. Some people have been eating poorly for years; so even if it takes a few months to set up a good eating program, ultimately, you'll be better off.

The goal of this three-meals-a-day program is to establish a normalized eating schedule that will affect your lifetime eating habits. You can still modify your caloric intake by reducing the caloric content of your meals and choosing low-calorie snacks, but you should be able to eliminate the need to overeat or binge by reducing the physical and psychological feelings of deprivation.

During this program, you can exercise as often or as seldom as you like. Initially, the focus is on food consumption. Once you are routinely eating three meals a day, you'll most likely find that as a by-product of normalized eating your exercise habits will also become more normalized. Without the need to work off a binge or to compensate for slipping on an excessively restrictive diet, your exercise workouts should now be time enjoyably spent working toward general body fitness. The information in chapters 7 and 8 will help you set new fitness goals in your exercise program.

Food Diary. A food diary is another mode of binge control. Its goal is to help you determine if your eating patterns are affected by your moods. If, after completing a food diary, you find that indeed they are, you should then use the remedies suggested for dealing with depression- and anxiety-based exercise addiction detailed in chapter 4.

To begin, you should plan to make no changes in your

daily schedule of eating and exercising for two weeks. During this time keep a list of every piece of food that goes into your mouth. Also keep track of what you're doing and how you feel just before eating (whether a meal, a snack, or a binge) and then record your mood shortly afterward. Do this before and after exercising. This kind of record keeping will give you a clearer view of how mood affects your need to binge and exercise. If you note a pattern of anxious or depressed feelings just before eating and/or exercising, you'll find it easier to break the binge-purge hold if you use the information in chapter 5 to help you seek and find the cause of those negative feelings that seem to push you into aberrant eating and exercise patterns.

Jannette, whose experience with bulimia was discussed earlier in this chapter, agreed to try this approach to help control her eating disorder. After four days her diary looked like this:

MONDAY

7 A.M.

coffee and a hard-boiled egg
Before: Feel good; eager to go to work; had a good weekend.
After: The same.

NOON

lettuce salad and boiled, skinless chicken leg
Before: Getting work done. In control.
After: Still hungry.

7 P.M.

one hard candy
Before: Hungry; want to lose five pounds; I'll go to the gym.
After: The same.
After exercising at the gym: I feel great. Won't eat dinner.

TUESDAY

7 A.M.

coffee and plain yogurt
Before: A little tired.
After: Same.

NOON

dry tuna and plain popcorn
Before: Worried about work; tense.
After: A bit better; still tense.

7:30 P.M.

fifteen creme-filled cookies, one quart ice cream, one bag
pretzels, eight Hostess cupcakes
Before: Thinking about a new electrocardiagram machine at
work. Feeling nervous and scared I'll have to operate it
tomorrow. Felt like having a snack.
After: I feel so angry and fat. How could I do this again. I'm
so disgusted with myself. Feeling so sleepy.

12:30 A.M.

Took a nap, now I'm ready to exercise. I know it's late but I feel
too guilty and fat to put it off until tomorrow. I'm going to
run around the neighborhood for at least forty-five min-
utes.

1:30 A.M.

I feel much better, glad I didn't put off this run until tomor-
row. I know I won't let myself eat so much again. Tomor-
row I'll get back on my diet.

WEDNESDAY

7 A.M.

coffee
Can't eat. Still feel fat, but so much better since I ran last
night.

NOON

spinach salad

Before: *So hungry, but have to control myself. Not too nervous.*

After: *Feel better. Will get right back to work.*

7:30 P.M.

lettuce salad and apple

Before: *Tired and hungry.*

After: *Will go to gym since I binged last night. Everything in my life would be perfect if I didn't binge.*

After exercising at the gym: *Feel good, but tired. Did an extra aerobic class.*

THURSDAY

7 A.M.

coffee and bagel

Before: *Tense about work.*

After: *Enjoyed bagel. Still tense.*

10:30 A.M.

two doughnuts and coffee

Was at a meeting and felt so anxious that I'd have to speak about new EKG machine. Ate snack feeling out of control and angry at myself. Will get back on diet and skip lunch.

Jannette had followed this same progression of events almost every other day for the past five years. During that time she had never connected the stress of her job to her eating problem. She was surprised to realize that her eating disorder had worsened just a few months after she landed her job. Although, as explained earlier, going off to college was the impetus that set off the cycle, the stress of her job and her feelings of insecurity and incompetence intensified it and kept it in motion. When Jannette looked back over her diary entry above, she saw for the first time that her worries about work started the binge and, most important, the binge and subsequent exercise purge completely overshadowed her original worry about operating a new piece of medical machinery. Once the binge was over, she turned her emotional energies toward self-loathing and guilt; after the exercise purge she felt good again without ever having to address her work problems. Unfortunately for Jannette, the stress of her job would soon show its face and two days later she would again use food to smother it.

The causes of bulimia are varied and complex; many of its victims cannot trace their problem to a specific emotional stress—but some can. The food-diary remedy will help you determine if your eating problem has a stress trigger. If it does, the remedies for depression and anxiety factors explained in chapter 4 can be implemented to deal with the underlying problem. Once the emotional problems are recognized and addressed, you may find that your need for binging and then exercise purging will ease by itself, or that other coping strategies suggested in chapter 4 can be initiated to take the place of eating. Or, you may find that the three-meals-a-day plan explained above will work in conjunction with the identification of negative feelings to reduce and eventually eliminate the need for binging and exercise purging.

There are times, however, when binging by itself or combined with exercise or purging becomes too big a problem to cope with alone using the strategies explained above. In these cases there are various kinds of professional help that can assist the bulimic in attaining a normalized eating schedule. These include:

Individual psychotherapy. The emphasis in this kind of therapy is on the problems of the past and present that might explain why one is binging. These sessions involve the affected individual and a trained psychotherapist who specializes in eating disorders.

Behavior therapy. This therapy is usually practiced with a psychologist who uses specific techniques to retrain the affected person. It is a highly structured approach that may use a variety of techniques to help the eating-disordered patient regain self-control.

Medication therapy. Psychiatrists have discovered that some antidepressants help decrease or eliminate the urge to binge. These medications work on the level of the brain's neurotransmitters. Some find total relief with the medication; others find it a useful adjunct to other kinds of therapy.

Group psychotherapy. This kind of therapy usually consists of a group of five to ten people, all with eating disorders, who are led by a trained group psychotherapist. Together they examine the feelings behind binging, as well as offer support in the attempt to overcome the problem.

Overeaters Anonymous. This is a twelve-step program modeled after Alcoholics Anonymous. In group meetings, participants offer support to overcome the problems of overeating and they seek an alternative method to deal with the feelings that lead to binging.

Central to any of the above kinds of therapies is the goal of factual education. Bulimics need to understand the problems that accompany extreme dietary restraint and the physiological consequences of both binging and restricting in conjunction with exercise. All sessions should be conducted in a supportive and nonjudgmental atmosphere.

ANOREXIA ATHLETICA

The anorexia-exercise link is difficult to resolve on one's own. Although the prognosis for a cure is good, most often anorectics (both those who do and do not use exercise as part of their weight-control regimen) need professional intervention. This is because, unlike bulimics, anorectics do not want to give up their behavior. They find it a necessary part of their existence and fear extreme weight gain if they resume normal eating and exercising. Moreover, anorectics often have distorted body images, believing (and seeing) themselves as fat when, in fact, they are emaciated.

Anorectics are often successfully treated with family or group psychotherapy and behavior therapy. Individual psychotherapy is also used. When anorectic athletes lose weight or refuse to eat or stop exercising excessively, they often come dangerously close to starvation and require hospitalization where these therapies are implemented.

To find the therapy best for you, you should seek an evaluation with a therapist who specializes in eating disorders. This therapist will take into account individual factors, such as how thin you are, how entrenched you are in this behavior, what other problems may be involved with your eating disorder, and how deeply rooted the problem may be. With this information, the therapist can determine which kind of therapy is most appropriate for you. You can locate a therapist who specializes in eating disorders by calling one of the organizations listed in Appendix B.

7

The Facts About Healthy Exercise

Exercise, when sensibly undertaken, is the activity most likely to improve your health. It can help control weight, reduce depression and anxiety, increase self-esteem, lower risk of cardiovascular disease, ease lower back pain, and promote strength, endurance, and flexibility. But when abused, exercise has the potential to injure, promote pain and fatigue, cause heart problems, compound emotional problems, and frustrate and disappoint the exerciser.

To avoid this negative side of exercise, most exercise addicts need to redefine their beliefs about the purposes of physical activity. The purpose of exercise is certainly *not* to maintain an obsessive-compulsive personality, avoid life's problems, supplement pathological eating patterns, mask problems with self-acceptance brought on by a poor body image, or hide from the pain of anxiety or depression. When exercise is used for these purposes, it is less productive and works against its natural purpose, which is to promote good mental and physical health.

Healthy exercise produces numerous benefits for the exerciser. It makes the heart and lungs more efficient and the muscles more capable of utilizing oxygen—thus increasing the maximum capacity of the muscular and circulatory systems. Also it burns calories and improves appearance, general health, work capacity, and the ability to combat fatigue. Although exercise can do all of these positive things, you might not gain the benefits you seek if your program is not well planned or paced.

We know it's difficult for exercise addicts to change their exercise schedules because it leaves them vulnerable to the psychological problems that led them to exercise addiction, and because they believe that their excessive regimens are appropriate and keep them "in shape." Changing them, they fear, would not only upset their emotional state but their physical appearance as well. That's why before you can change your program of exercise from one that fosters health problems to one that improves your health and well-being, you need to know the facts about what exercise can and cannot do, and how it can work with or against the body. This information will help you understand why your present routine may be unnecessary and even counterproductive.

PRINCIPLES OF FITNESS

Excessive exercise programs often ignore the three basic components of fitness: adaption, overload, and progression. All physical activity aimed at promoting good health should be based on these principles.

ADAPTION

The human body has the capacity to adapt to increasing degrees of activity if it is progressively conditioned to work harder. It can respond to the need for additional energy and strength without accompanying discomfort if it is given time to make changes in the way it functions. As the body adapts to physical demands, the circulatory system has to send more blood to active muscles and decrease blood supply to organs not in immediate need of a full blood supply. The nervous system must push more muscle fibers into action; the muscles need to convert carbohydrates into energy, and the heart has to pump, without excess strain, more oxygenated blood to working muscles. The bones, tendons, ligaments, and connective tissues will all become stronger as physical adaption takes place.

Unfortunately, many individuals exercising for reasons other than the pursuit of good health push the body too hard, too fast, and too often. They come to believe that the physical discomforts of chronically sore muscles, constant shortness of breath while exercising, cramps, and general fatigue are earmarks of dedication. If your exercise routine *regularly* leaves you feeling sore and stiff the next morning, you are asking your body to do more than it has had a chance to adapt to.

OVERLOAD

The process of adaption works on a principle called overload. To understand this concept, consider thirty-seven-year-old Jack who wants to add cycling to his 1.5-mile-a-day swimming regimen. He wants to be able to ride thirty miles of hilly terrain without suffering fatigue or muscle cramps. But on the first day out, after finishing his morning swim, Jack found himself exhausted after cycling only eight miles. Two days later, despite his sore leg and hip muscles, Jack was able to ride those same eight miles, after his swim, with less effort and fatigue. Each day thereafter, Jack found that his 8-mile route became easier as his body adapted to the need for extra strength and energy. When this happened, Jack was able to overload his newly conditioned muscles safely and push them to adapt even farther to 13 miles. When these 13 miles can be cycled with relative ease, he will be ready to overload again and push to an even greater distance.

Overload conditioning improves physical performance because it gradually pushes the body to a more efficient level of functioning. In endurance training, for example, overload of a particular muscle group leads to improved oxygen transport and utilization, thus increasing performance and aerobic capacity. Optimal conditioning can be achieved by manipulating combinations of the frequency, duration, and intensity of one's training. Exercisers must be careful, however, not to push beyond their top level of tolerance, which would violate the principle of progression.

PROGRESSION

What would happen if Jack decided to cycle a brisk thirty miles on his first attempt? Even though he is in shape from his daily swimming routine, his body could not adapt to this rapid progression in overload because cycling uses different muscles and body movements. His body would be unprepared for the sudden physical demands and would respond with pain and fatigue. It's not that Jack can't cycle thirty miles; it's simply that his body can't adapt so quickly.

Jack can improve his performance by increasing the frequency of his cycle workouts, or their intensity, or their duration. But he cannot expect to increase all of these aspects of training at once. Jack will do well if he concentrates first on duration. If Jack gradually increases his mileage (but not his intensity or frequency), he will see rapid changes in his body's ability to adjust to increased demands. He will be able to push his eight-mile outing to a ten- or eleven-mile one in just a few days. Then he can stay at the ten-mile rate while he ups the intensity of his cycling by increasing his speed.

However, Jack, and many exercisers like him who want to increase their exercise time, may be tempted to ignore the laws of progression when he discovers that as the body's adaption capabilities level off, the jump from an easy ten-mile ride to an easy fifteen-mile one will probably take more effort and longer training time.

Exercise addicts, in general, tend to feel they can bypass these principles of fitness because as the tolerance characteristic of addiction kicks in, they need to keep extending their routines to maintain the initial benefits. Those who are forced to change their form of exercise due to injury or circumstance often expect to pick up a new mode of activity at the same level of proficiency they had established in their previous program. These exercisers repeatedly risk injury and discouragement because the human body must be allowed to increase the intensity, frequency, and duration of exercise according to the principles of adaption, overload, and progression. If the body is not given this opportunity, it is prone to discomfort, fatigue, and risk of injury.

A telltale sign of an exercise program that works against the body's needs is in the degree of breathlessness that accompanies the workout. If you cannot talk in an intelligible manner during the course of your exercise session, you are overexerting and exceeding your body's capacity to supply the oxygen necessary to fuel the demands of your body. Contrary to the excessive exerciser's creed, excessive shortness of breath is not a sign of a "good" workout. A "no pain, no gain" credo can easily cross the line from beneficial to destructive.

A rough measure of your healthy exercise limit is found in your pulse rate when taken during and immediately after your workout. Your average maximum capacity is a pulse rate of 220 minus your age. Therefore, the *maximum* capacity of a twenty-five-year-old is 195. (220 − 25 = 195.) To measure your pulse and compare it to your maximum capacity use your index and middle fingers (not your thumb; it has its own pulse) and feel for rhythmic pulsing at either the radial artery found on the palm side of your wrist in the hollow just below the thumb, or at the carotid artery on either side of the neck about one inch behind the Adam's apple. Count the pulse beats for ten seconds and then multiply that number by 6 to find your pulse rate per minute. If twenty-five-year-old Lisa measures her pulse during an aerobic workout and finds it to be 26 in ten seconds, she would multiply this number by 6 and find that her 156 rate is below her maximum limit of 195.

To adhere to the principles of adaption, overload, and progression, Lisa should exercise at only 75 percent of her maximum capacity. Seventy-five percent of her maximal rate of 195 beats per minute (bpm) is 146 bpm. The fact that her 156 bpm rate is over her ideal target rate, combined with her abdominal cramps and breathlessness, indicates that Lisa's workout is overly intense and beyond what she needs from her aerobic class.

Lisa can adjust her exercise program to gain its benefits by changing either the intensity or the duration of her workout. The best and safest results can be obtained with a moderate intensity and long-duration workout. If Lisa follows her aerobic program at a slower pace, her one-hour workout will probably keep her pulse rate at the 75 percent ideal range. If

Jack cycles at a slower pace, he'll more readily and safely complete his thirty-mile goal. Exercisers can obtain similar results if they increase the intensity but decrease the duration. If Lisa likes to work out at a fast pace, she should stop after thirty minutes or forty-five minutes; if Jack likes to cycle for speed, he should lower his mileage goals. Total energy expenditure is the product of intensity × duration, so the two can be adjusted reciprocally.

EXERCISE AND BODY SIZE

We know that body weight, muscle tone and mass, and clothing size can be affected by exercise. However, the way calories, fat, and muscles react to exercise depends on a variety of factors that make simple equations such as "a one-mile run consumes 100 calories" misleading. (A calorie is the amount of heat released when a specific amount of work is done.) To attain weight-loss goals through exercise, you need to know how the body's metabolism works with its calorie and fat supplies to respond to exercise.

METABOLISM

The physiological mechanism responsible for the variability in the rate of weight gain and loss is called the metabolism. Each of us has a basal metabolic rate (BMR), defined as the number of calories needed to maintain bodily functions while at complete rest. A person with a low BMR burns calories slowly and needs less food to gain weight than a person with a high BMR who burns calories quickly and can eat more food without gaining weight. More calories are needed by the high BMR than the low BMR to breathe and keep all the biological functions going. BMR is basically genetically determined, but factors such as age, weight, body structure (including height, width of bones, and structural irregularities), as well as the level of fitness, do affect our metabolism. Knowing about these variables will help you achieve your exercise goals and avoid the dangers of working against yourself.

Twenty-seven-year-old Bob's experience with weight loss is typical. Bob is a five-foot ten-inch computer salesman who wanted to lose 30 of his 210 pounds. He teamed up with a 260-pound coworker and began an exercise and diet regimen that included cutting 500 calories a day off his usual intake and cycling eighty miles a week. For the first month, the results were dramatic. Bob lost 3 to 4 pounds each week and after one month had dropped two clothing sizes. As it will for most overweight beginners, exercise gave Bob's metabolism a boost so it was burning calories more quickly than it had been able to do without exercise. He was also losing weight due to the fluid lost in perspiration.

Delighted with the success of his fitness program, Bob decided to continue at the same pace for another month to drop the last fifteen pounds. While Bob continued to lose weight during the following month, he was disappointed with his slow progress; he was now losing only one pound a week. Bob was frustrated and confused because at this rate it would take another four months to reach his goal. "What happened!?" he wondered.

What happened to Bob eventually happens to all exercisers. Following the principle of homeostasis, the body's metabolism adjusts to the new physical and dietary schedule and slows its initial metabolic boost; the body then returns to a "normal" rate of functioning at the increased level of energy consumption and decreased level of caloric intake.

When Bob first began cycling, he was overweight and he wasn't in good physical shape so he had to work quite hard; these factors increased his metabolic rate. This physical effort, which burned calories quickly, combined with the decrease in caloric intake to give Bob the initial dramatic results. But as Bob became more fit, he cycled more easily through the route that had earlier caused him to struggle and strain. He no longer needed to burn the same amount of calories and so his weight loss slowed. For Bob to sustain weight loss at the level of his initial benefits, he'll need to increase the intensity and duration of his exercise routine. But even then, his metabolism will eventually adapt and slow down again. This speed-up/slow-down cycle will continue as long as Bob persists in adding to his mileage goals. Bob will have to adjust to the fact that his new exercise and diet plan will lead to slower and slower weight loss, ending at the point of his target goal, where his weight will stabilize and his weight loss will end. Unless Bob recognizes this metabolic dilemma, he may be driven to excessive workouts with disappointing results.

Bob was also disappointed because his exercise partner, following an identical regimen, lost more weight than he did. This was bound to happen because his friend weighed more to begin with and therefore was working with a different BMR. Simply put, people who weigh more use more energy per unit of exercise time. Looking at the chart in Appendix C, you'll see, for example, that a person who weighs 110 pounds and walks at three miles per hour will burn 4 calories per minute, but someone weighing 185 pounds will, at the same pace, burn 6.6 calories per minute. As the pace increases, the calories burned increase as well. The 110-pound walker burns 6.1 calories per minute at a four-mile-an-hour pace, but the 185-pound walker burns 10 calories. Another example of how weight affects the amount of energy expended is seen by comparing two runners. A runner of 110 pounds running an eight-minute mile will burn about 650 calories after an hour of running, but only 420 calories if he or she slows down to a twelve-minute-mile pace, and 870 calories if the pace is increased to a six-minute-mile pace.

It is true that heavier people use more energy while exercising, but keep in mind that all calorie formulas are only estimations. Many other factors influence exactly how many calories are burned during each exercise session. The environment itself can drastically affect caloric expenditure. Running on a smooth surface, for example, burns fewer calories than running on cluttered or inconsistent terrain. Cycling with the wind burns fewer calories than cycling against the wind. Rowing with the current burns fewer calories than rowing against it.

Another factor complicating the "one-mile run consumes 100 calories" equation is the metabolic afterburn that some exercisers experience. Afterburn is the caloric consumption that continues after exercise is finished. It is based on the "oxygen debt" that occurred during exercise and the "repair" mechanisms that enable the body systems to regain an equilibrium.

During and after a physical workout, your body needs additional oxygen. That's why the real volume of air you breathe while exercising is eight to ten times above your resting level and remains at this elevated rate for some time after exercise has stopped. At times as much as 10 percent of the recovery oxygen is used to reload the blood as it returns from the muscles after exercise. Another 2 to 5 percent is needed to restore the oxygen dissolved in body fluids and necessary to the myoglobin-oxygen complex in the muscle itself. Oxygen is also needed to replenish the energy-producing molecules and to convert the lactic acid produced during exercise back to glycogen. The heart, too, works harder during exercise and needs additional oxygen to recover its normal pace. Tissue repair and the redistribution of the ions that are part of muscle physiology ($Na+$, $K+$, $Ca+2$) also require the body to burn extra energy after exercise. Hormones that are involved in exercise (such as epinephrine, norepinephrine, thyroxine, and growth hormone) continue to maintain their elevated levels in the body's metabolic rate during the recovery phase. This process of oxygen recovery burns calories and contributes to the afterburn effect.

Afterburn occurs after even mild exercise, but it is most significant after exceptionally intense workouts that raise the body's temperature by as much as 5.4°F. This elevation of body temperature stimulates the metabolism, which leads to an increase in recovery oxygen consumption, thus burning even more calories. This process will continue as long as the body temperature remains elevated—sometimes hours after the exercise period is finished.

Although the exact extent of the afterburn effect is controversial, it does exist and can increase the metabolic rate long after you shower, go home, eat, and fall asleep.

Individual basal metabolic rates, body size, environmental factors, and afterburn will all affect the number of calories you burn during your workouts. This makes it difficult to calculate exact numbers, but the basic facts you should know about your metabolism and exercise are:

• Heavy people burn calories more rapidly than thin people.
• Beginner exercisers burn more calories than experienced ones.
• Initially, exercise will speed up the body's metabolism;

eventually, however, it will return to its normal level of functioning even though the exercise routine continues.

• Generally after age thirty-five it takes fewer calories and more exercise to avoid putting on weight. This is because with age the body's daily energy requirements decrease and the metabolic rate slows down.

Because of these factors, if Peg, who is overweight; Jane, who is a newcomer to exercise; Jeff, who has been running regularly for two years; and Mike, who is forty-five years old, all run the same one-mile route, they will burn a different number of calories.

Muscle and Fat

For exercisers, body weight alone can be an inaccurate indicator of fitness. Although Bob is determined to lose another fifteen pounds, he may, in fact, reach his goal in body size and fitness long before he loses the weight. As explained above, although an exerciser's metabolism slows as it becomes more efficient at doing the same amount of work, physical activity will continue to help the body lose inches by increasing muscle tone. Tight muscles give our bodies a firm and healthy appearance. However, they also *add* pounds to our body weight because muscle is denser than fat. As muscle replaces fat, you will lose inches and appear trimmer but could actually *gain* weight! This fact is so commonly overlooked by weight-conscious individuals that people like Debbie, whose weight-loss problem is described in chapter 5, are actually fined by the administrators of weight-control programs for not losing weight even though they may drop a full dress size. For exercisers, the mirror and clothing size are better indicators of changes in body size than is the weight scale.

CALORIES AND FAT

Because many exercisers don't know about the relationship between muscle, fat, metabolism, and weight, they assume that when they stop losing "easy" pounds they should exercise harder to regain their initial weight-loss benefits. This, too, can lead to disappointing results. Running, cycling, dancing, and swimming harder or faster may burn more calories, but this is not necessarily the same as burning more fat.

The difference between burning calories and burning fat is a matter of energy production and consumption. The food we eat is transformed and conserved as potential energy in adenotriphosphate (ATP) molecules. The energy we expend comes from the breakdown of ATP to adenodiphosphate (ADP) molecules; this process breaks a chemical bond which releases energy and enables our muscles to move.

Energy is released by burning, or metabolizing, carbohydrates, fat, or muscle. The intensity and duration of exercise determines which energy source is activated. If your body demands instant energy for intense activity (as happens, for example, when you jump into an aerobic class without a warm-up period) the ATP energy supply is rapidly consumed and the body will look to the carbohydrate-based glycogen-lactic-acid system to supply energy. (Glycogen is a carbohydrate that is stored in muscles and provides energy and burns calories in the initial bursts of intense exercise.) When you exercise intensely the glycogen system is activated immediately without waiting for extra oxygen. This is called anaerobic energy—meaning "without oxygen." But because glycogen is stored in limited amounts, high-intensity exercise will soon deplete this energy supply and you'll begin to feel fatigued as lactic acid is produced as a waste product during the anaerobic conversion of glycogen to energy. Lactic acid is irritating to the muscles, hence the fatigue and pain or discomfort.

If you continue largely anaerobic exercise after the pain and fatigue set in (perhaps believing "no pain, no gain"), your body will be forced to break down muscle to make more glucose for energy (this happens through a process called gluconeogenesis). This is a self-defeating and potentially harmful biochemical state that will cause fatigue and muscle cramping without contributing to the goal of weight loss.

On the other hand, when muscles are exercised slowly and moderately, they rely on an aerobic energy supply that feeds oxygen to the muscles. This kind of oxygen-based energy system enables exercisers to build cardiovascular and muscle-strength endurance. As endurance builds and the duration of the exercise program is progressively extended to stay within the limits of the exerciser's tolerance level, the muscles will begin to utilize stored fat for energy. This is the most productive and efficient way to lose weight because fat represents the greatest source of potential energy and weight loss—in the normal-weight individual, fat stores consist of about 90,000 to 110,000 calories.

During brief periods of exercise, equal amounts of carbohydrates and fat are metabolized for energy. If the exercise session continues at a steady pace for one hour or more, the carbohydrate stores will become depleted and the body will increase its use of fat to fuel its energy needs. That's why, to burn more fat, your exercise program should involve moderate intensity and extended duration. When you work out at a reasonable pace for an extended period of time, you'll contribute to your efforts to lose weight more significantly than if you exercise fast and hard for a shorter period of time. If you find yourself breathless and cramping while exercising, that's a signal that you're working anaerobically and not optimizing your body's ability to burn fat.

BODY COMPOSITION

The goal of healthy weight-loss programs should be to increase the body's ratio of lean mass (bone, muscle, and water) to fat. Exercise can help you do this, but you need to know what percentages are best for you. Of course, too much fat is not attractive or healthy. Excess fat makes it harder for a person to move around; it forces the heart to work harder to circulate blood, and it puts strain on the ankle, knee, and hip joints. On the other hand, too little fat is dangerous because it is needed to store energy, insulate nerves, protect vital organs, and help normalize many aspects of metabolism. A well-planned weight-loss program combines diet and exercise to find the middle ground where lean mass increases and fat decreases to the point that is most beneficial to your appearance and overall health.

A desirable fat content range for average females is between 16 and 23 percent of the total body weight. Males should generally maintain a fat content range between 11 and 18 percent. However, many elite athletes, especially runners, cyclists, dancers, and gymnasts whose performances can be compromised by excess fat, often lower their body fat far below the "normal" level. Your ideal fat level depends on your fitness goals.

Remember the commercial jingle for a breakfast cereal that said "You can't pinch an inch on me"? This advertising campaign implied that *anyone* who could pinch an inch of body fat was overweight. Certainly, many slim and trim adults were confused to find that they could pinch an inch of body fat on several areas of their bodies (especially on the waist, inner upper arm, and thigh). Were all these people really out of proportion in their lean mass/body fat ratio? The answer is: It depends.

If athletes or serious exercisers are in training for competitive events, they might want to lower their percentage of body fat to the bottom-line level where it is difficult to find an inch of loose fat. If, however, they are working out for more normalized weight-loss and overall fitness goals, those who can find an inch of body fat are not necessarily out of proportion. Few of us, in fact, could or should lower our body fat percentage to the level of elite athletes. World-class female runners have 10 to 11 percent body fat levels; male world-class athletes have even less. Neither reflects a sensible goal for people whose primary occupation is not athletics. But because it's difficult to determine how much body fat is the right amount, many exercisers establish excessive schedules in order to reach the fuzzy goal of "correct" body composition.

Body-fat percentage is especially difficult to determine because it's not reflected in the reading on the bathroom scale and is not broken down on weight charts like the Metropolitan Life Insurance Company Weight Table. So all of this information about exercising to attain an ideal lean mass/fat ratio means little unless you have some way of measuring fat. If you want to find your present fat percentage and set an appropriate goal for total body composition, you'll probably have to look for a coach, trainer, or doctor who has the ability to evaluate a person's body-fat composition accurately. To find such an expert, your best bet is to call a sports-medicine center at the local college or hospital.

Body-fat evaluations are done in one of two ways. An underwater weighing test can be used to determine body-fat levels. In this test, the individual is submerged under water and the body-fat composition is determined either by weighing the water displaced by the person's body or by directly weighing him or her under the water. An easier method is skinfold analysis. In this evaluation, specially designed calipers lift folds of skin and underlying fat from various body sites. The thickness of these skinfolds, measured in millimeters, is calculated into a formula to determine the percentage of fat in the tissue. These tests have become a common component of preseason conditioning programs for professional athletes and, most recently, for serious exercisers as well.

Exercisers who do not obtain a professional analysis of their body-fat levels must decide without this input whether or not to lose more weight in the pursuit of perfect body composition. Ultimately, this decision must come down to common sense and good judgment and fit in with the healthy exercise goals you set in chapter 8. But before you decide that your health and physical performance might be improved by a reduction in body fat, you should know that some people have body types that maintain high levels of body fat despite even the most vigorous exercise programs; also, that the hormone estrogen makes it difficult for women to lose body fat beyond a certain point, and that your childhood weight may influence your present proportion of body fat.

BODY TYPE

Some people have an inborn propensity to be bigger than our culturally prescribed ideal body image. Thirty-four-year-old Pam has been fighting this tendency for nearly twenty years. She still remembers her frustration back in high school when she and her best friend would diet together. "Trish and I would follow identical diets (grape-fruits, instant drinks, or whatever the going fad was at the time) and she would always lose more weight than me!" Even now, Pam struggles with her body's resistance to weight loss. Recently she confided, "I think it's important to my career to have a slim body, but I'm really getting tired of this uphill battle. I diet and exercise myself into a frenzy, but I just can't seem to get the fat off my thighs and hips. I can usually get my weight down to about 130 pounds, but after that it's like my body slams on the brakes. It's so hard to get below that point, and even when I do, my thighs stay fat and eventually all the weight comes right back on. I think I was born to be a fat-thighed 130-pound singer."

Pam was being facetious, but actually she was nearer the truth than she realized. It seems that each of us *is* born with a genetic tendency toward a certain body type. Some families run tall and slim, others tall and large; still others pass on genes for a short and stocky build, and some for normal height but large buttocks or thighs. This isn't to say that it's futile for some people to try to lose weight. But it does mean that not everyone can look like Cher or Patrick Swayze, that some exercisers will have to work harder than others, and that a weight-loss program should be structured with realistic goals in mind.

Many people, like Pam, diet strictly and exercise regularly but still have a great deal of trouble dropping below a certain point. Some researchers believe this is because each of us has an individual "setpoint" of basal metabolic rate. According to this theory, a combination of factors, including metabolic response, conspire to set a proportion of body fat that's natural for each of us.

To calculate your setpoint, think of the weight to which you eventually return after dieting. When Pam manages to diet down to 115 pounds, her body rapidly makes its way back up to 130 by making her hungrier for the calories she's missing. To stay at 115 pounds, she must radically cut calories, and this makes her tired and irritable. Her metabolism adjusts to an apparent setpoint at 130 pounds by burning fewer calories, thus making it easier to put on weight.

Your setpoint isn't absolute. You can bring your weight down below the setpoint and keep it down, especially if you're aware of the phenomenon and therefore stay vigilant in your diet and exercise regimen. You can even lower your setpoint by keeping your weight below it for a substantial period of time. Gradually, your metabolism may adjust to your new weight and weight-loss routine by returning to its higher rate of functioning. This will allow you to balance out at a lower weight.

However, the majority of dieters and exercisers will find this diet plateau a frustrating hurdle in their attempts to lose weight permanently. To compound their disappointment, many, like Pam, will learn through trial and error that it is almost impossible to reduce fat deposits on specific body sites. Inherited genes and fat cells will most likely keep Pam's thighs heavier than she wants them to be. Diets do not work on a spot-reduction basis, and, although exercise can tone and tighten flabby muscles, they cannot change the genetically determined distribution of fat cells. Exercisers who are not aware of this often become frustrated and increase the intensity, duration, and frequency of their routines only to find themselves chronically fatigued, often injured, and possibly exercise addicted, and *still* heavy in certain areas or unable to eat the foods they would like without putting on weight. For these exercisers, the most difficult part of setting exercise goals is in accepting that their body's setpoint may be established at a weight they don't perceive as being "perfect."

There are many factors involved in healthy weight-loss

exercise programs. Chapter 8 will help you use the information about exercise and your metabolism, muscles, fat, body composition and type to set healthy, realistic, and attainable weight-loss goals.

EXERCISE AND PHYSICAL HEALTH

THE CARDIOVASCULAR SYSTEM

The cardiovascular system is a complex entity made up of muscles, valves, chambers, blood vessels, arteries, and veins that pump oxygen-rich blood to every part of the body. Its rate, rhythm, and total functioning are dramatically affected by exercise because all muscles involved in sustained activity require additional oxygen to work. The greater the demand for oxygen, the greater the demands on this system.

Although self-stimulated, the heart is a muscle like other muscles in that it works best when exercised regularly and properly. Too little exercise increases the vulnerability of the heart if it is suddenly overworked or exposed to other stresses. But to exercise more than is necessary to achieve cardiovascular fitness is in no way discernibly better for the heart than moderate exercise, and in fact, at worst, leaves it vulnerable to arrhythmias and even cardiac arrest when unable to supply the oxygen demanded by persistently intense workouts. Because the heart is so integrally involved in your exercise program, you should know the facts about cardiac fitness before you head to the gym, pool, or roadways. (If you are over forty-five years old or have cardiovascular problems, you should consult your doctor about having a stress test before diving into the pool, pounding the pavement, or discovering the wonders of computerized bicycles, rowing machines, and the like.)

Exercises that demand muscle action for extended periods of time depend on a continuous supply of oxygen for sustained energy; this oxygen is delivered to the muscles through what's called the aerobic system of energy production. How well this system works depends, largely, on the heart's ability to pump oxygen through the bloodstream to the working muscles. Although medical researchers have found that how effectively a person's heart can supply oxygen is an inherited trait, most people need aerobic conditioning to reach their inborn upper ceiling of aerobic capacity (called VO^2 max).

Aerobic conditioning is part of all exercise programs that require cardiovascular endurance and that use large muscles (primarily those in the legs) vigorously and continuously, as in running, exercise-walking, swimming, and cycling. This kind of conditioning helps the heart and the entire circulatory, respiratory, and muscular systems improve the body's ability to turn oxygen into energy. Exercise causes a number of bodily changes that facilitate this process.

• As exercise causes muscles to grow larger (hypertrophy) and stronger, extra blood vessels develop to increase the amount of oxygenated blood that can be delivered to the muscles.

• Red blood cells increase the efficiency with which the blood vessels carry oxygen to the muscles. As the red blood cells do this, they also increase in number, thereby increasing the body's ability to fuel the muscles with oxygen and thus energy.

• As the body is trained to take in more oxygen with each breath, the lungs respond by enlarging their surface area where oxygen is picked up by the red blood cells.

• Aerobic training continually exercises the chest muscles as they move the diaphragm in and out to take in and expel air. Strong chest muscles deliver more air to the lungs with each breath.

These four bodily changes help exercisers bring more oxygen in with each breath and more efficiently distribute it with each heartbeat. This has been shown to contribute to longevity because as the heart adapts to the raised demands for output, the coronary arteries become larger and healthier; this happens because there is a decreased danger of clotting and an increase in the stroke volume (the amount of blood pumped out on each stroke). The output in nonexercisers is increased only if the heart beats faster, but that causes cardiac strain. Simply put then, in those who exercise regularly the heart's power to pump without strain is greatly increased.

High blood pressure, excessive weight, physical inactivity, and anxiety are four common factors that put us at increased risk for heart disease. Each one is positively affected by exercise. Most exercisers know this but may not know what kind of exercise is most beneficial or how much is necessary to reap optimal benefits. This is especially true of exercise addicts.

Heart disease ran in thirty-year-old John's family. His father and grandfather both died in their forties of sudden massive heart attacks. Two years ago, John's doctor encouraged him to modify his risk factors for heart disease. Since then John has lost ten pounds, stopped smoking, and begun a strenuous daily workout that now includes two hours of either running or tennis, followed by an hour workout on Nautilus machines.

According to consistent findings of several research studies, John is overdoing it and wasting a great deal of his time. The most recent and largest study out of the Institute for Aerobics Research and the Cooper Clinic in Dallas has found that the greatest health gains are attained by those who move from being completely sedentary to moderately active. The authors of this study say this can be accomplished by walking a half hour to an hour a day at a fast but comfortable pace. Those in this eight-year study of 10,224 men and 3,120 women who were classified as "most fit" were subjects who worked out regularly and intensely, running perhaps as much as thirty to forty miles a week. Surprisingly, they gained little significant health advantages over the moderately fit group. In view of these findings, exercisers like John who strive for cardiac benefits through excessive exercise routines can reduce the duration and frequency of their workouts without forfeiting good health. This fact is especially important to exercise addicts who protest that they exercise excessively for health reasons. The medical community says this just isn't necessary.

Sample exercise programs to increase longevity that are recommended by the American College of Sports Medicine are detailed in chapter 8.

MUSCULAR SYSTEM

Because all modes of exercise involve physical activity, by definition exercise strengthens the muscular system. We all know that active muscles grow strong, but as an exerciser you need to know how strong muscles can help you achieve your fitness goals and what happens to your muscular system when it is subjected to overly frequent, intense, or abusive workouts.

Although all healthy exercise programs enhance the muscular system, if you are a serious exerciser, you might also be involved in some kind of program aimed specifically at

strength training (also called resistance training). Today, free
weights (such as dumbbells and barbells) and/or resistance
equipment (such as Nautilus or Universal equipment) are
common in virtually all gyms and spas. In fact, the American College of Sports Medicine recently suggested that not
only aerobic training but resistance training is important for
physical health. Without a doubt, individuals who train for
strength are healthier and have a competitive edge over
those who don't, but the recognition of the correlation between improved strength and improved health and performance is a relatively new one. Not long ago, it was believed
that strength training for women was a waste of time and
was counterproductive for men. It was feared that women
would seriously hurt themselves seeking nonexistent benefits, and that additional muscle mass would make male
athletes and exercisers muscle-bound, thereby reducing
their flexibility, speed, and ease of motion. However, recent
research has found just the opposite to be true. In addition
to improving muscular strength in males and females,
proper training can actually increase flexibility, enhance
speed by improving the muscle fibers' ability to produce
anaerobic energy bursts, and add to the fluidity and range
of body movement. Muscular strength also reduces the risk
of injury and decreases injury recovery time. Especially
appealing to health-conscious exercisers is the fact that exercise (when coupled with strength training) can actually fore-
stall the natural deterioration of muscle tissue. Although age
inevitably causes a reduction in muscular strength, stamina,
and posture, regular exercise can arrest this process and
give exercisers a livelier and less injury-prone existence in
later years. Moreover, a few recent reports have detailed the
advantages of increased muscular strength and mass attained through resistance training even by people in their
seventies and eighties.

Although increased muscular strength can improve physical health, exercise that pushes muscles too far, and even strength training itself, can be harmful. Exercisers commonly hurt themselves by ignoring the rules of adaption, overload, and progression (page 130). If you attempt to train too strenuously, too frequently, or with too much weight or resistance, you open yourself up to muscle strains, back sprains, muscle inflammation, and debilitating muscle soreness. Muscles should be pushed only to the point of momentary failure and no further. At that time, the exercise should be terminated for a recovery period of thirty to ninety seconds. Otherwise, the underoxygenated muscles can lose strength and rip—leading to a strain in the muscle itself or a failure at a nearby joint or tendon. When muscles are sore or fatigued there is often compensation—instead of using a fatigued arm and shoulder muscle, you incorrectly use your back, putting yourself at risk for a serious strain or even a pulled back muscle. Most exercise addicts cannot cut back, change, or stop their exercise routine once they are injured, further aggravating any injury. Exercising muscles that have been overworked certainly does the body more harm than good.

To reap the benefits rather than feel the pain of strength training, you should follow the basic safety rules of strength training, which include working with a partner/spotter, working the same area no more than every forty-eight hours, and lifting multiple repetitions of no more than 80 percent of your maximum capability. You should exercise each muscle to the point of momentary failure, but that failure should occur after no fewer than eight or more than fifteen repetitions. Failure at higher weights with lower repetitions builds bulk more than strength, and lower weight at higher repetitions will not continue to increase strength, but it will maintain muscle tone. Knowing and using good weight-lifting form is imperative because incorrect body alignment can cause serious strain and injury to other parts of the body. You should also carefully plan your training sessions in ways that don't conflict with the physical demands of other forms of exercise. A runner, for example, should not train muscles for strength and run on the same day. If you lift weights *before* you run (or cycle, or dance), tired leg muscles from squats or other leg exercises can make your hip and knee joints less able to offer the support you need. This invites injury. If you lift *after* you exercise, your circulation can be severely stressed and you can become fatigued and prone to injury.

Some exercise addicts are prone to weight-lifting abuse when they develop an "I can top that" mentality. If you try to break your own or someone else's record every time you work out, or if you regularly try multiple repetitions at your maximum capability, you can injure yourself. This, of course, runs counter to the goals of healthy exercise programs that leave you energized and healthy, not exhausted and hurt.

Strength training can improve the health and athletic performances of both male and female exercisers, but it is especially important for females to know from the start what training can and cannot do for the body. Strength training can improve a woman's state of muscle strength, but the absolute strength of females in the general population is only about two-thirds that of males. It can also tone and firm muscles so that the body appears fitter and healthier. However, strength training cannot increase the size of a female's muscles beyond a certain point because women do not produce the male androgens (testosterone, for example) necessary to build muscle mass. Females can mimic male muscle growth only if they use anabolic steroids—synthetic forms of testosterone. Although the dangers of such drug use far outweigh the advantages, some female, as well as male, exercisers use steroids because their desire to develop the perfect body and/or physical performance far overshadows the value of good health.

As a part of normal functioning, the body produces from cholesterol many kinds of natural steroids. They are a group of powerful hormones, including the male sex hormone testosterone, which is produced naturally by the testes. Synthetic steroids were developed in the 1930s in an attempt to build body tissue and prevent the breakdown of tissue that occurs in some debilitating diseases.

Although the Food and Drug Administration has since found that anabolic steroids do not effectively reach those particular goals, the drugs are approved and legally prescribed for treatment of certain types of anemia, specific kinds of breast cancer in women, hereditary angioemedema (a type of allergic reaction to some insect bites and foods), severe asthma, and other medical problems. But even when used for appropriate medical reasons, there are serious side effects. Moreover, after even fairly short-term use, there is a kind of physical dependence and steroid use must be carefully tapered off or the body's own production of steroids is affected.

Steroids are potentially injurious to health and even deadly when used nonmedically to enhance body size and physical performance. It is believed that these drugs were first used to enhance athletic performance by the Russians in 1954, when Soviet athletes dominated many international sports events. To remain competitive, in the late 1950s many American athletes followed suit. Today, steroids are widely abused by professional, amateur, high school, and even junior high school male and female athletes, as well as exercisers who seek bigger muscles and superior physical performance.

The extent of steroid abuse is unknown because nonmedical use is illegal and exact numbers are impossible to gather. But as college, professional, and Olympic teams begin to require steroid testing before competitions, the number of athletes using steroids is coming to light. The most celebrated case in recent years is that of track star Ben Johnson, who was stripped of his 1988 Olympic gold medal in the 100-yard dash when his steroid test came back positive. On the football field Brian Bosworth, a University of Oklahoma All-American, was barred from the 1986 Orange Bowl game because he tested positive. In 1987, the National Football League, recognizing the problem, set down rules calling for steroid testing in training camps and requiring players who test positive to be sidelined for thirty days.

As steroid use by notable athletes continues to make headlines, it becomes clear that these drugs are no longer confined to gyms where obsessive bodybuilders secretively shoot up in the bathrooms. Steroid abuse has crept into the entire fitness arena and is practiced in posh health spas, fitness centers, and local gymnasiums.

The question often asked is, "Why would talented, physically active people, many of whom would never think of smoking cigarettes or abusing alcohol or illicit drugs, take steroids?" A piece of the complex answer lies in the nature of athletics, which places great emphasis on body composition, weight, and appearance. Athletes and exercisers are sometimes tempted to alter their strength and size to improve their performance, impress their peers, and make them better than their opponents (or merely equal if they believe their opponents are taking the drugs). At first they see only the positive effects: a sense of euphoria, an aggressive and vigorous attitude, larger muscle size in less training time, and increased amounts of energy and speed.

What is also clear, however (and probably familiar to many steroid users themselves), is the negative body changes that steroid abuse can cause. One such body change actually causes exercise-related injuries. It has been found that steroid users have an increased chance of causing injury to muscles, tendons, and ligaments. Although steroids strikingly increase muscle strength and mass, they do not strengthen the muscle supports—the ligaments and tendons. When muscles get too strong for their supports, they are prone to injury and do not heal as well or as quickly as they do when they have developed naturally.

Also, "roids," "juice," or "gas," as steroids are called, cause dangerous side effects in one-third to one-half of the people who use them. (These numbers may be higher, but the long-term effects on users are still unknown.) Steroid use stimulates the hypothalamus area of the brain, which in turn affects other areas of the brain and body—particularly the pituitary gland, the testes, and the female reproductive organs. In males, this can cause decreased sperm production and a reduction in the size of the testes. This can lead to testicular cancer, infertility, and/or sterility. Male athletes may also notice femalelike breast tissue development. Female athletes who abuse steroids may notice the development of malelike pattern baldness and facial hair growth, as well as an extreme deepening of the voice and a decrease in breast size. Steroid use can also cause a side effect that mimics the symptoms of a pituitary-gland tumor. This condition, known as acromegaly, increases the width of bone and connective tissues, which causes grotesque feature changes on the body and face. These side effects may be transient during the period of steroid use or they may become permanent conditions.

Steroid abuse has other far-reaching effects. These synthetic hormones can cause an adverse effect on the body's production of high-density lipoproteins (HDL). These are a form of cholesterol that *decrease* the risk factors associated with the dangerous low-density lipoproteins (LDL). LDLs are a form of cholesterol associated with heart attacks; without full production of HDLs, an individual is at increased risk for heart attack. Steroids also endanger the long-term health of people who are already in a compromised state because they are anemic or have sickle-cell anemia. Steroid use will aggravate these preexisting problems and may eventually cause fatal liver or kidney disease. Steroids also cause psychiatric illness such as serious depression, as well as full-blown psychosis, known as "steroid psychosis" or "roid rage."

The chart below lists these and other physical side effects attributable to steroid use. In addition to these bodily changes, users may also suffer psychological problems such as mood fluctuations, nervous tension, irritability, hostility, aggression, sleep problems, delusions, and even suicidal tendencies. Obviously, steroids are not the wonder drug they at first seemed to be. Although the positive effects of steroid use may tempt a serious exerciser, the negative side effects, along with the reversal of the extra weight and muscle that occurs when the user stops taking the drugs, should make it obvious that steroids have no place in a healthy program of exercise.

Some Physical Side Effects of Anabolic Steroid Abuse

Acne
Breast development in males
Cancer of the liver
Cholesterol increase

Clitoris enlargement
Death from cardiac causes
Decreased sperm count
Decrease in women's breast size
Dizziness
Edema (water retention)
Frequent or continuing and sometimes painful penile erection
Headaches
Heart disease
Hairiness in women
Increased blood pressure
Jaundice
Kidney disease
Liver disease and tumors
Male-patterned baldness in women
Menstrual irregularities
Muscle cramps
Nausea and vomiting
Oily skin and hair
Prostate enlargement
Sterility
Swelling of feet or lower legs
Testicular cancer

Human growth hormone is another substance that has the potential for abuse by athletes and exercisers. Growth hormone controls the development of tissue and has been successfully used to treat dwarfism. It has recently attracted attention because it seems to alter the body's fat-to-muscle ratio by causing new muscles to grow. A recent study has found that in elderly people, growth-hormone replacement (to only the level present in the average forty-five-year-old) leads to a drastic decrease in body fat and a matching increase in muscle volume. Weight lifters and other athletes have begun illicit use of growth hormone in pursuit of artificial size and strength. Surprisingly, large numbers of parents who want their sons to be star football players are also pushing doctors to prescribe growth hormone for them. Unfortunately, using growth hormone also potentiates the growth of tumors. Like all quick and easy paths to greater size, strength, and accomplishment, the risks significantly outweigh the gains.

THE SKELETAL SYSTEM

It is believed that muscular contractions around bone can stimulate the bone to conserve its structural minerals and affect its strength and density. A recent three-year study found that subjects in the inactive group lost 3.3 percent of the minerals in their bones, while the active group gained 2.3 percent. In addition, the bones of the inactive group thinned by 2.6 percent, while the active group's thickened by 1.7 percent. These findings support the results of medical research that found that the bones in the playing arm of a tennis player can be 35 percent bigger than the same bones in the nonplaying arm.[1]

Exercise is good for the skeletal system, but our bones can be damaged by excessive or abusive programs, especially high-impact ones. (High-impact exercises are those which repeatedly pound or jar the body.) While running or doing aerobic dance, for example, the feet hit the ground with great force, and this shock must be absorbed by the feet, ankles, shins, knees, hips, and lower back. Most adults can safely do high-impact exercises on a regular basis if they wear well-cushioned shoes and work out on soft surfaces like grass or carpeting rather than asphalt or hardwood floors built over a cement base. The exercise addict, however, who continuously, persistently, and without concern for the initial pain does high-impact exercise is most prone to overuse injuries that include shin splints (responsible for 10 to 15 percent of running injuries), stress fractures, tendonitis, periostitis (inflammation of the membrane over the bone), and some knee and hip injuries.

Because addicts are often unwilling to change or reduce their exercise schedules when injured, many continue to abuse the skeletal system. Some make exercise work against its natural purpose to promote good health and turn it, instead, into a potentially debilitating habit that will eventually leave them with serious injuries requiring drug treatment or even surgery. The leg, for example, is prone to such injury, especially when one leg is longer than the other. Quite commonly, people are born with a significant leg-length discrepancy. Excessive exercise will put more strain on the shorter leg, causing the skeletal system and the slightly longer leg to compensate with a twist of the hips or the pelvis. This imbalance and its consequences increases the risk of injury.

The skeletomuscular system certainly benefits from a healthy exercise program. However, if you are addicted to exercise, it is likely that your excessive or overly intense routine is more harmful than helpful to the development of both your muscles and bones. As you rework your exercise program with the suggestions in chapter 8, you'll find that a stronger and healthier skeletomuscular system is a natural by-product of all normalized fitness programs.

THE NERVOUS SYSTEM

Although stress is often viewed as a mental-health problem, we include it here under physical health because the nervous system's response to stress is a physical one. Consider encountering one of your stress triggers (anything from a traffic jam to a run-in with the boss to a screaming infant). What are the physical characteristics of your body's reaction? As your nervous system sends the distress signal to your brain, your breathing and heart rate increase; then your blood pressure rises and your muscles tense. You're set for what's called "fight or flight." In earlier eras, the difference between bringing an animal home to eat and being eaten by the animal was the ability to react quickly to danger. As a consequence, the body was required to prepare for action at a moment's notice. To do this, adrenaline is released, breathing becomes faster and shallower in order to bring more oxygen into the body quickly. The heartbeat increases to push that oxygen and increased blood sugar through the bloodstream rapidly. And the blood flow is redirected from the internal organs and the surface of the body to the deep muscles, which need more energy to prepare for the fight. Those who had the quickest stress-response systems survived threatening situations and, as Darwin explained, became our ancestors. Although our ancestors' stress response, designed to promote the physical activity of fleeing or fighting, helped them to survive, it is in some ways an archaic and potentially dangerous response unless you are actually faced with danger.

You don't need extra oxygen directed to your deep muscles when you're caught in a traffic jam or hear your baby crying, yet it still happens. Your body prepares you to fight, but most often you have no physical foe. So what happens? Your heart beats rapidly, your blood pressure rises, your muscles tighten, all without a physical outlet, which, depending on each person's genetic vulnerabilities, can lead to such physical problems as ulcers, headaches, heart palpitations, backaches, rashes, colitis, allergies, asthma, heart disease, diabetes, and (as suggested by recent research) even cancer.

Exercise gives us a way to channel these physical responses and avoid bodily harm. Studies have confirmed that regular exercise lowers readings on such stress indicators as neuromuscular tension, resting heart rate, and some stress hormone levels. The stress-reduction benefits of exercise are so well known that a 1987 survey by the editors of the professional journal *Physician and Sportsmedicine* found that 82 percent of the 500 primary-care physicians polled regularly prescribed exercise to depressed or anxious patients.[2]

The stress-reduction capabilities of exercise are well documented. But it may not be as clear to exercisers what kind or level of workout is most likely to relieve stress and how much is necessary to obtain relief. Because the fight-or-flight response sends oxygen to the body's large muscles, aerobic-based exercise that requires sustained endurance and elevated pulse rate most effectively relieves the muscle tension and high blood pressure caused by stress.

It's true that daily life is full of stressful situations and that exercise can be the ideal antidote. If you exercise to achieve this benefit, chapter 8 will help you set up an effective exercise program and will help you recognize the fine line that separates a general stress-reduction program from one based on pathological stress avoidance.

SPECIAL HEALTH CONSIDERATIONS FOR FEMALE EXERCISERS

Because females are anatomically and physiologically different from males there are some special factors they should consider when planning a healthy exercise program. Some female characteristics actually put women at a disadvantage in the exercise arena. Because females don't produce testosterone they have less natural muscular strength. In addition, because they do produce the female hormone estrogen they have an additional proportion of body fat, which can, in some sports, compromise performance abilities. Females must also train longer and harder than males to achieve equal capacity for prolonged exercise. This happens because a girl's VO² max (the highest oxygen uptake possible during exhaustive exercise) levels off between ages eight and fourteen, but a boy's will continue to develop until sometime between ages sixteen and nineteen. As a result, adult males have 15 to 25 percent greater oxygen capacity than females. There is also a difference in the average level of hemoglobin and the resultant ability to transport oxygen to the muscles. Because males have a higher percentage of muscle mass they have a larger cardiac stroke volume and a naturally higher concentration of oxygen in the hemoglobin.

These factors give males the edge over females in competitive sports. However, these differences do not predispose women to failure or injury. Studies conducted by the military academies in preparation for accepting female cadets in 1976 concluded that although there certainly were discrepancies in athletic ability based solely on physiological and anatomic differences between the sexes, gross differences in performance capabilities were primarily the result of the lack of physical conditioning.[3] Although some early studies of injuries in female athletes reported a higher injury rate for females than for males, later studies that compared injury rates of *conditioned* female athletes found no increase over male athletes.[4]

Females, in the general population, may be less active and less conditioned than males because they are relative newcomers to the world of athletics. In fact, twenty-five years ago the Amateur Athletic Union prohibited girls under the age of fourteen from running races that were longer than a half mile, and no women ran the Boston Marathon until 1967. It was believed that if a girl ran long distances or trained too intensely when she was young, she would become infertile. It was also believed that menstruating females should not be physically active.

We now know these "facts" are not true at all. Females derive numerous benefits from physical activity that go beyond the normal health-promoting factors. Contrary to the myth that sports participation endangers reproductive function, it has been found that female athletes have fewer complications of pregnancy, shorter duration of labor, fewer cesarean sections, and fewer spontaneous abortions. The great majority of female athletes exhibit no change in their performance abilities during menstruation. Some women claim their performances are enhanced at this time of the month, and women who usually experience menstrual cramps note that moderate exercise relieves the pain. However, others feel they are unable to remain active during this time. Since no absolute statement can be made about athletic performance during menstruation, a woman's exercise schedule during this time depends entirely on personal feelings and desires. It has also been documented that exercise favorably increases the amount of calcium and calcium turnover in the body. This physiological change has been shown to delay the onset of postmenopausal osteoporosis to a significant degree.

As we have seen, excessive or too intense exercise negates the positive aspects of physical activity; menstrual disorders, too, can be directly related to intense physical activity. They may be caused by a combination of excessive training schedules, lowered body weight, reduced levels of body fat, and competition stress, which can lower the body's core temperature and influence the function of the ovaries and/or the hormonal release from the body or the brain.

A woman who has fewer than six menstrual periods in twelve consecutive months has a condition called oligomenorrhea; if she has fewer than two menstrual cycles in that same period she is suffering from amenorrhea. When these conditions are due to excessive exercise they are usually found in women who practice endurance sports like long-distance running. Although some female exercisers think it is desirable to skip the inconvenience and/or discomfort of monthly menstruation, oligomenorrhea and amenorrhea are signs of an unhealthy situation because they reflect an upset in the natural hormonal balance of the body. But because menstrual irregularities usually disappear when the exercise schedule is reduced the problem has long been considered benign. Recently, however, researchers at the Pacific Medical Center in Seattle found that there is physical evidence that the factors causing amenorrhea and oligomenorrhea have long-term and possibly irreversible physical effects. This study found lower bone density in fourteen nonmenstruating women ages eighteen to thirty-five—the mineral content of their vertebrae was at a level usually found in fifty-one-year-old women with low levels of estrogen. When these women regained their menstrual cycles, their bone density did not recover as rapidly.[5] It now appears that amenorrhea may set the stage for painful bone deterioration in later life.

It is also dangerous to ignore menstrual irregularities because other problems can be present with these same symptoms. Exercisers who experience menstrual changes should have a thorough medical exam to rule out hormonal problems, diabetes, connective-tissue diseases, pituitary tumors, thyroid underactivity, eating disorders such as anorexia nervosa or bulimia, and pregnancy.

EXERCISE AND MENTAL HEALTH

Exercise is embraced by many for its almost magical ability to create a general sense of well-being, improved self-image, and increased feelings of self-esteem. Among the general population, exercise is credited with relieving stress and promoting feelings of calm. Even those who suffer mood disorders such as depression and anxiety respond quite readily to a dose of physical activity. Although these effects are well documented, exactly why they happen is still being debated.

A CHEMICAL REACTION

Some researchers attribute the positive feelings after exercise to chemical changes in the body. The most popular theory focuses on the release of beta-endorphin, an opiate produced naturally by the body estimated to be 100 to 1,000 times more potent than morphine, another opiate. Like all opiates, beta-endorphin can increase one's sense of well-being and even reduce pain under certain circumstances. It's been found that the levels of beta-endorphin in the body respond to exercise. The levels of beta-endorphin can increase as much as five times beyond the baseline level (an increase of 500 percent) after just twelve minutes of warm-ups and vigorous exercise; it also continues to circulate at high levels for up to thirty minutes after exercise,[6] causing some to believe that beta-endorphin is responsible for the "high" feelings a workout can produce.

Other research scientists disagree with these findings for a number of reasons. There is no proof that beta-endorphin ever reaches the receptors in the brain that control mood and behavior. Built into the brain stem at the base of the neck is the blood-brain barrier, which regulates the exchange of fluids between the central and peripheral nervous systems. This wall of capillaries regulates the type and volume of chemicals allowed through. Although blood drawn from the forearm after exercise shows increased levels of beta-endorphin, there's no way of knowing if excess amounts pass through to the brain.

Peter Farrell of Penn State University has published research which concludes that mood elevation probably doesn't depend on beta-endorphins at all. Farrell conducted a study in which stationary-bike riders were given a dose of naloxone (an opiate-receptor blocker) before their session. Naloxone so effectively blocks these receptors that if it is given to someone high on heroin that person would lose the high feeling within five minutes. Despite the naloxone, the exercise subjects were less tense and anxious after pedaling than before they started.[7]

Other studies support these findings. One found that some people experience marked mood improvement after participating in activities equivalent in intensity to a college physical-education class. These researchers concluded it is unlikely that beta-endorphin is the cause of improved mental health in the vast majority of exercisers.

Many researchers now suspect there must be other reasons for the exerciser's high. Among other possible explanations is the possibility of an adrenaline reaction. Although there is some research supporting the argument that an exercise high is actually an adrenaline rush similar to that experienced in the flight-or-fight syndrome, this explanation is generally viewed as a bit too simplistic. Ample studies verify that fight-or-flight moods are often anxious and more similar to rage than the calm sense of well-being experienced after a physical workout. Direct evidence comes from studies conducted at Mount Sinai Medical Center in New York, where it was found that a half hour of steady exercise on a stationary bicycle (which is enough exercise to elicit an exercise high) did not notably increase the release of adrenaline or adrenaline-related neurochemicals.

The most plausible (but as yet unproven) explanation for the elated feelings brought on by exercise focuses on changing levels of serotonin in the central nervous system. Serotonin (also known by its chemical name 5-HT) is a regulatory neurotransmitter that controls levels of other transmitters (including adrenaline); it also regulates eating, sleeping, and other activities. The antidepressant Prozac increases the amount of serotonin available in the brain and induces feelings of well-being, lessens depression, and regulates appetite. If physical workouts alter serotonergic functioning, they could have the same effect as Prozac. It is important to note that the levels of serotonin do not seem to rise in direct proportion to increased levels of activity.

This information should give many exercise addicts reason to reconsider their workout programs. The multitudes who insist "I work out so long and hard because it makes me feel great! I wouldn't get the same lift if I cut back" have convinced themselves that extreme doses of exercise affects mental health. This does not seem to be true because it has been shown that people who work out only for brief periods of time also feel better and happier with themselves.

GETTING HOT

Another possible explanation for the calming powers of exercise is found in the thermogenic theory. This theory notes the relationship between muscular tension (an established measure of emotional state) and the rise in body temperature brought on by exercise. Our core body temperature can rise to 104 degrees with only fifteen minutes of aerobic activity and can remain elevated for several hours after a workout. This rise in body temperature relaxes the muscles, which then leads to a psychological experience of relaxation. Ronald Bulbulian, the director of the exercise physiology lab at the University of Kentucky, found that twenty minutes of mild exercise resulted in a 20 percent reduction in muscle tension.[8] This physical change might be expected to give an exerciser a calm mental response.

Researchers are quick to point out, however, that the same results can be obtained through passive warming sources such as a sauna or hot bath, suggesting that it is unnecessary for exercisers to use an extended workout to obtain muscle warmth and mental relaxation.

In the Eye of the Beholder

A rather simplistic, yet probable, explanation for the good feelings that many exercisers experience is the way physical activity affects one's self-image. Exercise is a socially admirable activity, and those who engage in it often see themselves as accomplishing something positive and worthwhile. Many who run, lift weights, swim, cycle, do aerobics, and so forth state that even a short workout makes them feel more fit, thinner, and more attractive. In fact, for people without severe body-distortion problems, exercise in all quantities improves their overall sense of self. Any activity that continually guarantees this kind of mental pat on the back promotes an improved self-image and, consequently, better mental health.

This theory addresses the variability in the mental rewards of exercise. It explains why some exercisers feel an emotional boost after only fifteen minutes of moderate activity while others claim to experience no elevation in mood unless they exercise vigorously for extended periods of time. Mara and her friend Debbie, both twenty-five-year-old teachers, are good examples of the self-image theory at work.

Debbie insists that it's impossible for Mara to feel any sense of elation when she runs for only a half hour three days a week. Debbie herself runs for at least one hour every day and still doesn't always feel "great" when she's finished. The difference in these mental responses to exercise probably lies in goals, expectations, and internal self-image. Mara is content with her moderate regimen and feels proud of herself for sticking to her schedule and doing something positive for her health. Exercise helps her feel good about herself; hence her elated feelings. Debbie, on the other hand, not only has set more demanding exercise goals but she doesn't feel she's thin enough even when everyone else thinks she looks great. If she feels sluggish during her run, runs at a slower than usual pace, or cuts her time short by even a few minutes she feels disappointed and guilty rather than pleased with herself for what she *has* accomplished.

This attitude toward goal setting and achievement can dictate how rewarding exercise feels and therefore what degree of mental peace and self-esteem is derived from physical activity. Exercise addicts who strive relentlessly for the ultimate "high" generally have a more difficult time attaining mental peace than those who practice a normalized program of activity with realistic goals.

8

Creating a New Exercise Program

Some excessive exercisers appear content with their addiction. They don't feel that it interferes with their normal daily functioning, and they have no desire to give it up. These people have no motivation to build a new exercise program. Many others, however—those who have asked for help, and the others whom we have met and surveyed, and those we've heard and read about—have found that exercise addiction, like other addictions, keeps them from living a full and well-rounded life. If excessive exercise patterns keep you from meeting your family obligations, career responsibilities, and personal goals and jeopardize your personal physical or mental health, it's time to create a new program of exercise.

This new program should be one that is no longer excessive yet still keeps you physically active and meets your personal exercise needs. Since these needs vary from person to person depending on age, weight, body composition, and long- and short-term goals, it's impossible to set forth a step-by-step exercise guide that will be just right for everybody.

As you begin building a new program, you need to ask yourself, "Why do I want to exercise?" Five healthy reasons might include: (1) cardiac health and longevity, (2) weight loss or maintenance, (3) improved mental health, (4) fulfillment of competitive drive, and (5) social contact and fun. You can more easily discard your addictive exercise patterns if you set one of these goals as your new target and aim to build a routine that will keep you involved in exercise that's good for you and leaves you time and energy for other things.

The following chart will help you determine if your favored form of exercise will help you meet your new exercise goals. You'll need a good match to succeed in your new program; so if you want to run to lose weight, the chart will let you know that the two are a good combination. But if you play golf to lose weight, the chart will point out that you're on the wrong track.

EXERCISE GOALS

Activity	Cardiac Health and Longevity	Weight Loss or Maintenance	Improved Mental Health	Fulfillment of Competitive Drive	Social Contact and Fun
aerobic dance	4	4	4	1	4
calisthenics	2	2	3	1	2
cycling (outdoors)	4	4	4	1	2
golfing	2	2	4	4	4
racquetball/ squash	4	5	4	5	4
roller skating	4	4	4	1	3
running	5	5	4	3	2
swimming	5	4	4	2	2
tennis (doubles)	2	2	4	4	5
tennis (singles)	3	3	4	5	3
weight training	2	2	3	1	3

RATING: On a scale of 0 to 5, 0 = none, 1 = trace, 2 = some, 3 = moderate, 4 = significant, 5 = superior

In order to break your addiction while continuing to exercise you'll need to do two things consistently: (1) be honest with yourself about what you really expect to gain from exercise, and (2) monitor your schedule to assure that it stays within comfortable limits and yet achieves maximum benefits. Let's say, for example, that you presently exercise for two hours five days a week because you want to maintain cardiac health. To achieve maximum cardiovascular benefits you need to exercise only three days for thirty minutes with your pulse elevated during this time. With this in mind, it may become obvious that your present routine is excessive and unnecessary. If, however, you decide not to change your schedule, you must at least admit that you're still really exercising for reasons other than cardiovascular health. To break your addiction, you'll need to rethink your goals, normalize your schedule based on the facts, and learn to enjoy the benefits and fun of moderate, healthy exercise.

As you reduce the frequency and intensity of your exercise to a healthier level, it's important to realize that you may occasionally slip back into your excessive habits. For example, you may have every intention of going out to take a reasonable run rather than the ten miles you have been forcing yourself to do, and find that you just keep on going. Or you may go to the gym with the intention of doing one Nautilus circuit and wind up also going to an aerobic class and doing the Stairmaster afterward. These slips are to be expected. Knowing that they are to be expected will prevent them from really throwing you off track.

Relapse prevention is an integral factor in the treatment of substance-related addictions; it is equally applicable to exercise addictions. To deal with relapses successfully, you must know that a slip is not a complete return to old behavior patterns. If you expect to be in control and never move backward, even occasionally, then, due to these unrealistic expectations, a slip may lead to discouragement and another relapse. Sometimes those administering a relapse-prevention treatment will actually suggest that people force themselves into a slip and then recover. If you do this, you may find that you are stronger than ever before. In any case, *slips will always happen*. To keep a slip from turning into a slide, you have to realize that small steps back are never indicative of a complete loss of all of your gains up to that point. Self-treating an addiction is a lot like life itself—often a journey of two steps forward and one step back—but the overall forward progression is most important.

When analyzing your relapses, you might notice that they are likely to occur as long as the issues that caused the initial exercise addiction remain unresolved. The factors that lead to exercise problems will lead you to seek exercise-related solutions. In fact, the frequency of lapses will tell you how well you're coping with the basic underlying issues. When the frequency of lapses starts to decline, the basic issues are probably being resolved.

GOAL NO. 1: IMPROVE CARDIAC HEALTH AND INCREASE LONGEVITY

The obvious signs of aging that plague sedentary people include the feeling of being "winded" after mild exercise (even after simply climbing the stairs), slow recovery from illness and injury, chronic fatigue, creeping weight gain, and muscle and joint stiffness. More insidious signs include the obstruction of arteries and veins, sleep difficulties, decreasing muscle tone, weaker bones, and the slowing of bowel function. Often, these physical problems can be greatly reduced or even eliminated through physical activity. Certainly, improved health and increased longevity are positive and attainable goals because there's no doubt that exercise can add more healthy years to your life. If you set this as your exercise goal, you can gain the maximum physical benefits possible with a moderate exercise program built on the following suggestions.

Activities, like weight lifting, which concentrate on building strength and/or muscular endurance, or calisthenics, which develop flexibility, can help you attain specific kinds of exercise goals and contribute to youthful feelings. But these kinds of exercises are less crucial in preventing life-threatening diseases and promoting longevity than those that enhance cardiovascular functioning. Cardiovascular exercises that best increase longevity are ones that are aerobic and use large muscles in rhythmic activities and that raise the heartbeat to a predetermined target rate. Long-distance running, jogging, exercise-walking, swimming, skating, cycling, rowing, and cross-country skiing are more likely to help you meet this goal than activities such as golf, weight training, calisthenics, or bowling.

The weight, size, and strength of the heart (which is an extremely complicated muscle) increase with long-term aerobic training. As a result of the larger left ventricle and the stronger contractibility of the heart muscle, there is an increase in the amount of blood that leaves the heart with each beat (the stroke volume). This increases the amount of oxygen available to the body and helps decrease blood pressure. Because of these positive changes, the heart doesn't have to work as hard during both exercise periods and everyday functioning.

The American College of Sports Medicine (ACSM), a professional organization of physicians, physiologists, and physical-education teachers, has published an exercise program that has been shown to give maximum physical health benefits. We find their recommendations to be ideal alternatives to addictive regimens and have used them as a base for the exercise programs below. The ACSM recommends workouts that raise your pulse rate to between 60 and 90 percent of the heart's maximum rate;

this rate is found by subtracting your age from 220. (The formula below explains how to calculate your target heart rate.) To obtain maximum cardiovascular benefits, this elevated heartbeat should be maintained through exercise for twenty to thirty minutes, three or four times a week.

Many exercisers mistakenly try to maintain good cardiovascular health by exceeding these guidelines. If you have been playing doubles tennis and lifting weights with machines six days a week for two hours each day, you may have been putting in a lot of time without gaining significant physical benefits because this exercise, while lengthy and partially aerobic, doesn't maintain the pulse elevation for long enough periods of time. You would come closer to reaching your goal with a twenty-minute pulse-elevating jog three days a week.

DETERMINING YOUR TARGET HEART RATE

1. Estimate maximum heart rate by subtracting your age from 220.
2. Find the lower range of your target rate by multiplying this number by .60.
3. Find the upper range of your target rate by multiplying the number found in Step 1 by .90.

For example:
If you are thirty-five years old, your target heart rate is:
1. $220 - 35 = 185$ beats per minute
2. $.60 \times 185 = 111$
3. $.90 \times 185 = 166.50$

In this example, the thirty-five-year-old exerciser has a maximum heart rate of 185 beats per minute. The appropriate aerobic training heart rate lies in the range between 111 and 166.5 beats per minute. (See the information in chapter 7 to review how to best count your heartbeats.)

It has been found that sedentary people can attain physical-health benefits from workouts that do not raise the heartbeat to this target rate. But seasoned exercisers do not continue to maintain cardiac functioning if their workout falls short of the ACSM recommendations. Any activity that does not maintain the heart's target rate for at least twenty minutes, or does so fewer than three times a week, may be fun or offer a competitive thrill but, according to the majority of exercise research, will not meet the goal of improving cardiac health or increasing longevity. There is some recent data that suggest that the twenty or more minutes of aerobic activity does not have to be continuous. A group of people doing three ten-minute sets of aerobic exercise improved their cardiac health to the same degree as those performing workouts of identical intensity for a thirty-minute stretch.

To many exercise addicts, this plan for attaining adequate cardiac benefits will appear too easy. You may wonder how this seemingly minimal amount of exercise time can do anything worthwhile. The answer lies in the results of numerous studies that consistently find that exercise programs that exceed the ACSM recommendations do not significantly increase one's life span. If you have set the attainment of physical health as your exercise goal, all you need to do is to create a program that follows the ACSM guidelines. If you find, however, that health improvement is your foremost reason for exercising and you genuinely enjoy longer workouts, you may want to decrease the intensity of your exercise after it exceeds the recommended three days of twenty- to thirty-minute aerobic, high-pulse workout. If this feels unsatisfactory to you, an honest review of your exercise habits will probably show that you're still exercising for reasons other than good cardiovascular health.

EXERCISE PROGRAM FOR CARDIOVASCULAR HEALTH

An Adequate Program. In order to receive adequate benefits for cardiovascular health, you simply need to engage in an aerobic activity for twenty minutes, three times a week. During this exercise time, keep your pulse rate at 80 percent of your maximum rate (as explained above). If you find that twenty consecutive minutes is hard or inconvenient, some research suggests that the same benefits can be obtained from two ten-minute blocks of exercise, three times a week.

A Better Program. In order to enhance aerobic conditioning and cardiovascular health, you can exercise more frequently or intensely. Push yourself harder for brief periods so that your heart rate may temporarily (for a minute or two) exceed the 80 percent level and then return to your previous level of effort (but do not fall below it). Stay at that training level for a period of time (two more minutes or so) and then push back up above the 80 percent level again.

At first you may need to push and then rest, but the goal is to push up the intensity level and then rapidly recover to the 80 percent training level. For example: While riding a stationary bicycle, bring your pulse up to 80 percent of your maximum rate. Then rapidly increase the revolutions per minute to further raise your pulse for a minute or two. Then fall back to recuperate at 80 percent of your maximum. Then increase again for another short burst. Then return again to your training level.

An Optimal Plan. In order to play certain sports at high levels of competence without undue cardiac stress, optimal aerobic conditioning is required. This level of conditioning is needed, for example, in order to ski an entire expert trail without stopping or to play a twenty-hit point in racquetball or squash. With a minor adjustment, the burst and recover process described above can help you reach this level of cardiac fitness. Accelerate the process of adaption by cutting back on the recuperative time between energy bursts. You do not need to extend the duration of your workout but rather shorten the time between the recovery and the next burst.

An Excessive Plan. Excessive exercise plans involve exercising for extended periods of time above the 80 percent level without any recovery periods. Forcing yourself to keep pushing when your pulse rate is at or over 90 percent is excessive and it does not produce *any* added benefit, but it does increase the risk of burnout, exhaustion, electrolyte imbalance, and traumatic cardiac events.

Once you are in peak condition, there is no additional aerobic benefit in exercising more than approximately thirty minutes, four or five times a week. So running fifteen miles four times a week will not result in a healthier cardiovascular system than running approximately five to six miles four times a week.

GOAL NO. 2: SUPPORT WEIGHT-LOSS OR MAINTENANCE PROGRAMS

Many find that the attraction of exercise is not just the possibility of increasing cardiac fitness but the more concrete satisfaction of feeling slim and trim. Before you set this goal of weight loss or maintenance, you first need to know about how body weight and exercise function together. Studies indicate that sustained weight loss (rather than immediate water-weight loss) occurs in weight-loss programs that combine moderate food control with moderate exercise. As already discussed, excessive dieting alone can slow the metabolism to a point that makes sustained weight loss almost impossible. The ideal weight-loss or maintenance program combines a moderately low-calorie, low-fat diet with a moderate aerobic exercise plan; this combination burns body fat, speeds the metabolism, and increases muscle tissue, thereby increasing caloric need. These should be the targets of your weight-loss goals.

Exercising to lose weight usually requires more time and effort than exercising to maintain cardiac health alone. As you become more fit, your body becomes more efficient. The higher your muscle/fat ratio, the more calories you burn in merely going through normal activities of daily living but the fewer calories you burn exercising relative to those you burned when you began. Your body has become a more efficient and well-tuned machine, so to increase actual weight loss you need to increase the duration, intensity, or frequency of your exercise program. Although this often establishes the groundwork for an exercise addiction, there are ways to maximize your weight loss without living only to exercise and to watch the numbers on the scale drop.

If you exercise to lose weight, you should establish a diet-exercise program that strives to shed only one to two pounds a week. Most dieters expect greater gains for their efforts, but as we've discussed, overly intense programs that offer initial dramatic results always level off.

If you exercise to maintain your present weight, you need to keep your caloric intake even with the energy you expend through all forms of exercise. Until you gain a feel for this balance, like those initially trying to lose weight, you'll need to watch how your calories relate to your exercise plan.

Although each individual varies somewhat in the way his or her body burns its calories, the chart in Appendix C will give you an idea of how many calories are burned by your mode of exercise. Until you have a feel for judging your daily caloric needs, you'll need to purchase a small booklet that lists the calories contained in the foods you eat in order to match your food-intake calories against your exercise-expended calories. As you do this keep these two facts in mind:

• To gain one pound of weight, you must eat 3,500 more calories than you burn.
• To lose one pound a week, you need to cut your food intake or increase exercise in order to burn an additional 500 calories a day.

This formula for burning calories is most accurate when calories are expended through activities that emphasize duration rather than intensity. You'll find that extended, rather than quick-burst anaerobic, activity will give you greater benefits in a weight-loss or maintenance program. That's why the kind of exercise you choose will dictate how your program should be scheduled. For example, Mike and Pat both want to lose a half pound a week without changing their already low-fat diets. (This may not seem like much to lose, but it's twenty-five pounds a year that will *stay* off!) In order to reach this goal, they'll each need to burn off approximately 1,750 calories a week through exercise. Because the "average" person can burn 500 calories running for one hour, Mike can meet his goal by running about one hour three times a week. Pat wants to take aerobic classes, so she'll probably lose her half pound per week by participating in three to five classes each week. (The exact number depends on the class itself and how active the rest of her day is.) If Pat and Mike are already exercising at these levels, they will need to *add* at least this much exercise in order to start to lose weight.

However, if after a few months on this schedule, Mike and Pat find that as their metabolisms adjust to their workouts, the half-pound-a-week goal will become more difficult to reach. Instead of adding more time (and risk a relapse into their addictive patterns), if they still need to lose weight they can challenge their bodies to burn more calories during their regular routine. Mike might change his route to include a more hilly area, or he might pick up his pace for a few minutes. Pat can choose a more challenging class, or she can cross-train with other activities or exercises. Both will find, however, that without changing a thing in the exercise programs the weight they have already lost will stay off.

Many exercisers find it easier to reach weight-loss or maintenance goals by cross-training. This is how nineteen-year-old college wrestler Dean keeps weight off. "My favorite exercise is running," he says, "but I don't have a lot of time in my schedule to add on more miles when I need to take off a few extra pounds. So when my usual routine loses its challenge, I do some biking or swimming for a while. I think this gives me a more well-rounded fitness workout and it seems to keep extra pounds from creeping up on me."

If you've set weight loss or maintenance as your exercise goal you have to accept that this process is a slow and gradual one. Gimmicks such as liquid diets, stimulant medications, protein-only diets, and other fad diets that promise quick dramatic results do not keep weight off or complement healthy exercise programs. You should also beware of weight-loss gains achieved while wearing a rubber sweat suit. Actually, these suits are not only ineffective, they are dangerous. Increased forced perspiration drops pounds in the form of water loss only; this can readily result in dehydration and the weight is regained when you drink fluids. Because rapid water loss upsets the body's natural cooling mechanism, it increases body temperature and can lead to heatstroke or heat exhaustion. Although fluid intake can bring the minerals and electrolytes back into balance, it also immediately returns the lost weight—so the additional effort is ultimately for naught. Although it may be exciting to lose an immediate two to four pounds after an especially sweaty exercise session, don't try to preserve that loss by restricting your fluid intake. If you don't rehydrate, the health problems associated with electrolyte loss are serious and potentially dangerous. Health and weight goals are both compromised by exercise programs that rely on excessive body sweat.

To many exercisers it is frustrating that weight loss is not always mathematically logical. Just because two hours of tennis can burn 800 calories, you can't assume that four hours will burn 1,600. As explained in detail in chapter 7, because the body's ability to burn calories is affected by many factors excessive exercise does not necessarily bring the hoped-for benefits. One pound a week is a healthy way to take off weight that is most likely to stay off.

As you plan and implement your new exercise program, you'll need to remember that we each have a unique metabolic rate. That's why two people with the same diets and exercise routines will not lose or maintain weight identically, or even work off inches to the same degree or in the same places. Also remember that some of us are genetically predisposed to have different body types than we would like. Setting realistic and healthy goals may mean acknowledging that although exercise can make you strong and fit, it may not be able to give you what you perceive to be the perfect body.

EXERCISE PROGRAMS FOR WEIGHT LOSS AND MAINTENANCE

An Adequate Program. In order to get adequate weight loss benefits from exercise and dieting, you can develop an exercise program that is equivalent to walking two miles in thirty minutes, three times a week. As you can see from the calorie chart in Appendix C, this program burns about 500 calories per week. This level of exercise will also speed up your metabolism to some extent and provide yearly weight loss of six to eight pounds.

You can also attain adequate levels of exercise-related weight loss if you change some of your daily habits. Walk up the stairs, for example, even if your office or apartment is on the eighth floor; walk the mile to work or to the store, and take walks with friends instead of meeting for an after-work drink.

A Better Program. A better exercise-related weight-loss program involves exercising every other day for the equivalent of running three miles (about twenty-five minutes). If you run three miles every other day, you will exercise about fifteen times per month and burn about 300 calories each time. This means that in one year you will exercise about one hundred eighty times, burn fifty-four thousand calories, and lose about fifteen pounds without changing your diet at all. Slight reductions in your diet (of perhaps 100 calories a day) will lead to an additional weight loss of ten pounds. Thus, exercising about twenty-five minutes every other day can bring about a twenty-five-pound per year weight loss or avoidance of weight gain.

An Optimal Program. It is possible to exercise the equivalent of running six miles per day, every other day, and double the weight loss or maintenance figures stated in "A Better Program" above. Running six miles with your pulse raised to its target rate is equivalent to about forty to sixty minutes of other aerobic activities. Exercises performed at this pace, every other day, will lead to a weight loss or avoidance of weight gain of about thirty pounds per year with no other life-style changes. This program will not produce negative exercise consequences and is unlikely, if your diet is adequate, to cause a reduction in the metabolic rate or starvationlike symptoms. Of course, exercising combined with decreased caloric intake will lead to even more weight loss.

An Excessive Program. Daily aerobic exercise of more than one hour per day (the equivalent of running fifty miles per week or more) does not give added weight-loss benefits. If one is dieting while exercising this much, there is a significant risk of injury (note the discussion of bone-mass losses associated with exercise in chapter 7). In addition, at this level of exercise there is notable risk of a metabolic slowdown which will cause immediate weight gain if exercise is interrupted due to injury or schedule problems.

See Appendix A for suggested readings on exercise and its relation to weight loss.

GOAL NO. 3: IMPROVE OR MAINTAIN MENTAL HEALTH

Without a doubt, exercise can have a positive impact on your state of mental health. Research has confirmed the ability of physical activity to lessen depression, anxiety, tension, and stress. Also, because mental health has a profound effect on physical health, exercising for psychological benefits can at the same time ward off somatically expressed psychological problems of colitis, asthma, ulcers, headaches, and heart palpitations. If you suffer from these mood disturbances and/or related ailments, their alleviation is certainly an appropriate goal for your new program of exercise.

Not only can exercise function as a preventive, many exercisers find that their workouts give them what's sometimes called an exercise "high." Striving to achieve this state is another reason for exercising, but one that is more likely to reinforce rather than break an addiction. Because many exercisers tend to believe that this psychological thrill is achieved only after long and intense workouts, they push themselves over that line that separates healthy from excessive exercise programs as they seek a mental boost. Some continue working on the far side of this dividing line because they have an overly inflated goal for their exercise high. They persistently seek intense elevation when the actual feeling they are more likely to attain is one of calm and relaxation.

Certainly there is a high that comes with exercise. You may, however, need to try many different things, like changing your kind of exercise or the time of day you exercise, to find what brings it on for you. You may love exercising to music, for example, and so the combination is effective for you. Or running five to six miles twice a week in the early morning may do the trick if you love watching the dawn. Although there is an exercise-related high, it remains poorly understood. Its occurrence surely depends not only on exercise but also on the exerciser's baseline mood state, as well as many other subtle factors. It is known, however, that you can best seek mental health through exercise by carefully noticing when, where, and how you most enjoy your workout.

If the improvement or maintenance of mental health is your only exercise goal, you can create an enjoyable program that offers the psychological benefits you seek, but remember: Exercise can't be used continually to avoid facing stressful situations, and your schedule must stay within the limits you set. (See "General Guidelines" on page 189.) Although addicts tend to believe that only intensive exercise schedules offer psychological benefits, this has been disproved in a recent study. When researchers at Florida State University compared novices, moderate 10K (6.2 mile) non-elite racers, and marathoners, they found the 10K moderate group to be the happiest. Members of this group scored lowest on all the measures of negative moods, and just as high as marathoners in vigor. Exactly why moderate exercisers reap the most mental-health benefits is not clear, but the researchers suggested that while novices may not exercise enough to enjoy the full emotional benefits, the marathoners' competitive drive gets in the way of stress reduction.[1] Although, obviously, some people who run 10Ks are less happy than others who run ten marathons a year, this study highlights the fact that, in general, moderate exercisers are more likely to use exercise to augment a life that has interests and rewards aside from exercise.

Although maximum psychological benefits appear to be attained at moderate levels of exercise, as an addict you might not feel satisfied exercising at this level. As your body adjusts to the physical changes and you crave longer workouts, you can get caught up in a cycle that pushes you to increase exercise time and intensity in pursuit not only of the initial positive physical responses but also of greater mental-health benefits. Whether or not you actually achieve greater benefits becomes secondary to the fact that the feelings of elation or accomplishment associated with aerobic sports tend to encourage greater and greater effort. You can counter this occurrence in your new exercise program by substituting some nonaerobic activities that are known to promote the feelings of elation that you seek. Activities such as snow and water skiing; wind-, body-, and board surfing; skateboarding; hang gliding; white-water rafting; parachuting; parasailing; and sailing are "thrill" sports that by their exciting nature guarantee a temporary boost in mood.

These activities are quite unlikely to cause or support an addiction for a variety of reasons. Thrill sports depend on specific weather conditions or seasons; they often require elaborate equipment; they can necessitate lengthy transportation, and for most people are impractical to do on a daily basis (except during a specific vacation time period). This makes these sports excellent habit breakers for people who tend to become too rigid about their exercise regimens.

At the same time, these activities can complement your regular exercise program. Although athletic in nature, most require skills that can be learned in a relatively short period of time. Also, they provide an excellent chance to use the skills that dedicated exercisers have already developed, including aerobic fitness, balance, muscle strength, coordination, and stamina. Thrill sports can make a desirable contribution to your new exercise program because they enhance skill development in ways that rarely become obsessive, all the while feeding your need for excitement, elation, and positive mental development.

GENERAL GUIDELINES

As you build a new exercise program to enhance your mental health, keep these guidelines in mind:

1. Consider a nonstressful mode of regular exercise. Choose activities that require little thought, are rhythmical,

continuous, and can be performed in pleasant surroundings without a lot of preparatory or participatory rigmarole. Swimming, jogging, and exercise-walking are often described as meditative and are healthy stress relievers.

2. With some degree of flexibility, schedule your weekly workouts in advance. This will keep you from falling back into the habit of using exercise to avoid stressful situations rather than learning to face them.

3. Follow the exercise guidelines for maintenance of physical health recommended by the American College of Sports Medicine (page 176). The members of this organization believe that maximum exercise benefits are attained by exercising at 60 to 90 percent of your maximum heart rate for twenty to sixty minutes, three to five times a week. This kind of moderate program will keep you in top physical shape and at the same time give you a steady dose of stress relief.

4. Complement your exercise program with other types of stress reduction strategies (some are explained in chapter 2). Because the mental effects of exercise are short-lived, lasting generally only two or three hours, it cannot, by itself, give you a continuous sense of calm.

5. Include alternate activities in your exercise program. As noted above, using thrill sports on a regular basis can lead to a boost in your mood with no risk of relapse in your addiction.

EXERCISE PROGRAMS FOR IMPROVED MENTAL HEALTH

An Adequate Program. As noted earlier in this chapter, exercising lightly (the caloric equivalent of a two-mile walk) three times per week can lead to significant increases in self-esteem. This level of exercise, if performed regularly and in a dedicated manner, can, indeed, provide adequate mental-health benefits.

A Better Program. Either aerobic or resistance (weight-lifting) exercise alone can lead to mental-health benefits— the combination of the two is even better. Aerobic exercise can help you feel fit (and therefore pleased with yourself), and it tends to be a rhythmic and calming activity. Resistance activities tone and tighten muscles and can lead to a more "desirable" body shape and personal pride. If you do a twenty- to thirty-minute aerobic workout every other day and on the in-between days do a reasonable resistance workout (eight to ten different exercises and eight to ten repetitions each), the benefits of relaxation and increased pride in muscular strength and tone will lead to better mental health. You can further enhance these benefits by exercising with a friend or while listening to music you enjoy.

An Optimal Program. "A Better Program" described above is a good exercise plan for exercisers looking for mental-health benefits. It can be enhanced by adding a wide range of exercise activities to the exercise schedule. In addition to basic aerobic and resistance activities, regular doses of skill sports, competitive sports, or thrill sports (added according to your own preferences and abilities) encourage maximum mental-health benefits.

An Excessive Program. Overly rigid adherence to a single mode of exercise will provide the least degree of mental-health benefits. In fact, an obsessive approach to get that high often associated with exercise often defeats the purpose. Because excessive habits cause anxiety over missed workouts, are too narrowly focused, and heighten the risk of injury and the resultant inability to exercise, they can *cause* more mental-health problems than they could ever cure.

See Appendix A for recommended readings for those seeking relief from depression, anxiety, or anxiety associated with obsessive personality traits.

GOAL NO. 4: SATISFY COMPETITIVE DRIVE

Many competitors become addicted to exercise as they struggle to become "number one" in their sport. Long hours of relentless daily practice boost accomplished tennis players like Ivan Lendl, golfers like Jack Nicklaus, and baseball players like Don Mattingly to the top. If you work out as part of a competitive training regimen, you'll need to sort out your priorities before you can deal with an addiction.

Generally, elite athletes make a commitment to their sport that supersedes all others because it is their *career*. They are fully aware that their workout time may interfere with family and social obligations (as do many career responsibilities), but it is a life-style they have chosen, and they are willing to accept the sacrifices it demands. If you are involved in this kind of all-or-nothing athletic routine, your workout *is* your top priority. In this case, your behavior is not an addiction but necessary in your pursuit of perfection. Elite athletes seem to find that they have total control over their workout schedules and can easily turn them off anytime intense training isn't necessary.

However, if you are a nonelite competitive athlete (meaning one who is not ranked in any sports circuit) and your workout schedule is wreaking havoc in other areas of your life, it's time to reconsider your exercise goals and competitive needs and create a more moderate workout schedule that will help you break your addiction but still satisfy your competitive drive.

Thirty-four-year-old Ron, for example, is a self-described "softball fanatic." Several years ago, he moved to a mild-climate state where he could play softball year round. Now, he plays in three different leagues so he can be on the field seven days a week. Ron loves the game because, as he says, "Every time I hit the ball, I can mentally watch my batting average rise. I'm the best batter in all three leagues and I intend to keep it that way." Ron thrives on the competitive atmosphere he finds in softball by keeping a careful tally of his stats; he can compete with the opposing players, with his own teammates, and even with himself. But after eight years of this demanding schedule, Ron is beginning to realize that his competitive drive has caused him to make sacrifices in other areas of his life. "I never date," he laughs. "No girl would put up with my ball schedule. And I know I could get a better job, but I've been afraid that I might have to work longer hours and then miss some games. I've been thinking that I should probably give this up."

Ron doesn't necessarily have to give up softball to break his addiction, but he will probably have to allow more time for other activities by dropping out of one or two of the leagues. This would give him more time for other things and still give him weekly opportunity for competition. Ron might also substitute a competitive sport or activity like squash, raquetball, or even job hunting that would satisfy his need for competition but take up much less of his time.

If you begin to create new outlets to break your addiction, you'll also need to schedule the newly created free time carefully. Ron can't successfully drop one of the softball leagues without assuring himself that he'll have something else of value to him to do with that time.

During this period of readjustment, you should also search to find a possible underlying reason for letting your competitive drive overshadow other important life activities. It may be that you need to prove yourself over and over again; perhaps you can pinpoint a psychological problem that compels you to win or see constant growth in your abilities. People who have low self-esteem may find an ego boost in the athletic arena. Those who have jobs that offer little opportunity for advancement may find a replacement for their diminished status through physical competitiveness. Some people (especially men) try to excel in sports to prove their worth to their fathers who may admire athletic individuals. Others caught in conflict-filled relationships may find an outlet for their aggressive feelings on an intensely competitive athletic field. Perhaps more than just fulfilling a need for competition, Ron's softball schedule feeds an obsessive personality or acts as an avoidance behavior. Chapters 2 through 6 will help you in your search. But if your needs are quite intense and you cannot uncover a reason for them, you may even benefit from professional intervention.

EXERCISE PROGRAMS TO SATISFY COMPETITIVE NEEDS

An Adequate Program. An adequate level of competition is often achieved by simply entering a single race or tournament. Entering, assessing your competence, being one of the competitors, and trying to win against people with your own general level of ability may be all that's needed to give you the amount of sports competition you crave.

A Better Program. Cross-training is required in order to perform "better" in competitive sports. (Cross-training also

helps exercise addicts overcome their problems with inflex-
ibility.) For example, if your sport requires endurance training (such as is needed in running), other endurance sports
like bicycling or swimming will help you train. Or if your
sport requires strength (such as needed in tennis) added
resistance training will improve your performance to a
greater degree than would merely increasing your sports-
playing time.

An Optimal Program. Optimal competitive functioning
demands consistent practice in your own sport as well as
regular and varied workouts that improve the varied components of your sport. If you want to be a more competitive
runner, you will need to run the distance you race at (10K,
for example), practice longer runs occasionally to build endurance, and do some interval training in order to improve
your ability to handle bursts of greater speed. You will
probably also want to do resistance workouts that focus on
the muscle groups that are key for your sport. Finally, when
practiced shortly before specific competitions, other types
of aerobic cross-training, such as jump-roping, cycling, or
swimming, will help reduce the risk of injury. You can
build this kind of optimal program that includes endurance, interval, strength, and aerobic training without
becoming involved in an excessive program. The sample
competitive training schedule in Appendix D illustrates
how one of our nation's top competitors trains without
becoming addicted.

An Excessive Program. Few people have the natural physical ability to perform at the professional or national championship level in *any* sport. For nearly everyone, simply
adding more workout time to an already maximal training
schedule is not likely to result in a major competitive win. A

daily regimen of running eight miles, in addition to weight workouts and two hours on the tennis court, will not make most people ready to challenge Stefan Edberg in tennis. Although it's clear that excessive training without exceptional natural ability will not make most exercisers "number one," the need to be more competitive is often the addicted exercisers rationale for working out excessively.

GOAL NO. 5: SOCIAL CONTACT AND FUN

Many people exercise for very practical reasons: "I want to stay healthy," some say. Or, "I want to lose weight," say others. Hopefully all exercisers find that while fulfilling their pragmatic goals they're also having fun, because the most effective exercise programs are those in which positive feelings are a natural by-product. There are some people, however, who exercise for no reason other than pure enjoyment. When this is the case, you'll have no trouble setting up a moderate program of exercise that you can enjoy and yet that won't interfere with other activities and obligations.

If you're honest with yourself, you'll probably discover that an addiction to exercise is not rooted solely in love of physical activity. Not one exercise addict has been able to declare truthfully that he or she finds "fun" in working out at inconvenient hours; during inclement weather; when injured, ill, or exhausted; and at the expense of other enjoyable and important life activities. Yet, eventually, all addicts do these kinds of things. Many excessive exercisers will admit, almost as a shameful secret, that at times they don't even like exercising. Some dread their 5:00 A.M. runs in the middle of winter; others drag themselves to the gym while still aching and exhausted from a bout with the flu, to avoid feeling guilty. Some even experience transient secret relief when it is impossible to work out for some reason. Although secretive, this is not surprising. Who actually enjoys running in temperatures of 98 degrees and 99 percent humidity, or in the middle of a sleeting rainstorm? Who could enjoy swimming a mile when every stroke is painful because of a shoulder bursitis? Or how could going to the gym at 6:00 A.M. every morning be fun when your boss has you on a project that kept you working until 1:00 A.M. for the last two weeks? All of these exercise situations are obviously unpleasant, but all are common stories from exercise addicts.

Fun grows naturally out of normalized exercise programs. These regimens don't push your body beyond tolerance limits, don't demand that you sacrifice personal or business relationships, or fill you with guilt and self-loathing when you miss a scheduled workout. Normalized programs are, by their nature, moderate. Also, fun exercise doesn't need to focus on only one activity; cross-training and substitutions can be easily accommodated to give the exerciser a well-rounded physical workout. So if you feel energetic, but it's snowing, you can substitute a swim at the gym or cross-country skiing for cycling. Or you can choose not to exercise at all on that day.

There may be a few individuals who appear to thrive on obsessive, excessive, self-abusive, and rigidly disciplined exercise routines. Their reasons for finding fun in this manner, however, are aberrant and extend far beyond what exercise can reasonably be expected to deliver. The remedy for such a problem lies in therapy with a professional and is beyond the scope of this book.

You can certainly set fun as your exercise goal if you are honest with yourself and vigilant in practice. Make sure your regimen is at all times pleasant, relaxing, self-fulfilling, moderate, and good for you. Then you can truthfully say, "I exercise just for the fun of it."

EXERCISE PROGRAMS FOR SOCIAL CONTACT AND FUN

An Adequate Program. An adequate level of fun can be attained by those who practice exercise activities that they naturally enjoy without stress or frustrating effort. It will be more fun to practice aerobic dancing than golf if you lack eye-hand coordination. Opportunities for social contacts while engaging in a fun sport can be easily found by planning your exercise schedule at times and in places where you'll see other people.

A Better Program. You can improve your chances of finding fun in your exercise program by following the "General Guidelines" for improving mental health through exercise suggested on page 189. Also, exercising in the same place, at approximately the same time, on the days you choose to exercise will enhance the opportunity to see and meet people you recognize and with whom you can most easily engage in conversation. If you find fun in competition, you'll also discover that you have a better chance of enjoying social contact if you enter competitive situations such as tournaments and races.

An Optimal Program. Joining a sports club will certainly optimize your opportunities for both social contact and fun. There are running and cycling clubs and aerobic classes that meet once or twice a week where you can work out with people who are also involved in the sport that you enjoy. Often, team sports promote more of the socialization you may be looking for; joining a league that plays softball, basketball, or even a club that sponsors matches of tennis, squash, or racquetball puts you in contact with people with whom you can share your sport and the enjoyment of some competition.

An Excessive Program.   Often those who are lonely will look to sports clubs, gyms, and athletic activities to fulfill all their needs for socialization. Unfortunately, if the only way you can find enjoyable contact with others is through your chosen exercise, you set yourself up for developing and maintaining an exercise addiction. If you are going to the gym and working out every evening and for a good portion of the weekend in order to meet people and chat, you should think seriously about why you are looking to exercise to take care of your social needs.

Epilogue

Throughout this book, we have tried to give you an in-depth and realistic look at exercise addiction. We've explored the ways exercise can take on the characteristics of a true addiction; we've dug into its roots to find why some exercisers get hooked, and we've offered nonaddictive exercise programs that are based on sound physiological facts. We have taken this (as far as we know) first venture into the heavily populated world of exercise addiction in an effort to give those of you who are hooked an objective look at the problem and a workable solution that will help you, once again, use exercise in healthy and beneficial ways.

We would be pleased to hear from readers who use the information in this book to reorganize their exercise schedules. Tell us about your successes, your problems, and your setbacks. We will not be able to answer your letters personally, but we will be able to use the information in our continuing study of exercise addiction.

Send your letters to:

Dr. Philip Harvey
c/o Simon & Schuster
1230 Avenue of the Americas
New York, NY 10020

Appendix A:
Recomended Reading

DEALING WITH DEPRESSION

David Burns. *Feeling Good: The New Mood Therapy*. New York: Morrow, 1980.

David Burns. *The Feeling Good Handbook: Using New Mood Therapy in Everyday Life*. New York: Plume, 1990.

DEALING WITH ANXIETY AND/OR OBSESSIVE PERSONALITY TRAITS

Claire Weekes. *Hope and Help for Your Nerves*. New York: NAL, 1990.

Claire Weekes. *Peace from Nervous Suffering*. New York: Signet Press, 1990.

DEALING WITH EATING DISORDERS

Jane Hirschmann and Carol Munnter. *Overcoming Overeating*. New York: Ballantine Books, 1988.

Steven Levenkron. *Treating and Understanding Crippling Habits and Obsessive Compulsive Disorders*. New York: Warner Books, 1991.

Marcia Germaine Hutchinson. *Transforming Body Image: Learning to Love the Body You Have*. Freedom, Calif.: Crossing Press, 1985.

Janet Polivy and Peter Herman. *Breaking the Diet Habit*. New York: Basic Books, 1983.

Michele Siegel, Judith Brisman, and Margot Weinshel. *Surviving an Eating Disorder: New Perspectives and Strategies for Family and Friends.* New York: Harper & Row, 1988.

DEALING WITH BODY-IMAGE PROBLEMS

Susie Orbach. *Fat Is a Feminist Issue.* New York: Berkley, 1978.
Susie Orbach. *Fat Is a Feminist Issue II.* New York: Berkley, 1982.
Susie Orbach. *Hunger Strike.* New York: Norton, 1987.

INCREASING FLEXIBILITY IN EXERCISE SCHEDULES

Dr. Michael Hamilton, et al. *The Duke University Medical Center Book of Diet and Fitness.* New York: Ballantine Books, 1990.
Dr. Kenneth Cooper. *The New Aerobics.* New York: Bantam Books, 1970.

Appendix B:
Resource Guide

BEHAVIORAL THERAPY

Many of the more serious problems discussed in this book are best treated with behavioral interventions. To find a behaviorally oriented therapist you can contact the Association for the Advancement of Behavior Therapy. This association has members who are psychologists, psychiatrists, and social workers. All members are interested in clinical applications of behavioral therapies. To obtain referral information you can call their New York office at 1-212-279-7970.

PSYCHIATRIC REFERRALS

Some problems that require professional assistance may also require treatment with medication and therefore necessitate consultation with a psychiatrist. To find a suitable psychiatrist you can contact the closest medical school and explain that you would like a referral from their department of psychiatry. We do not recommend having general practitioners prescribe psychotropic medication unless they are working in consultation with your therapist.

OVEREATERS ANONYMOUS

This organization applies twelve-step principles to issues regarding overeating. There is a chapter of OA in virtually every medium-size and larger town. Look in the phone book to locate one near you.

AMERICAN ANOREXIA/BULIMIA ASSOCIATION

This organization provides information, referrals, and self-help groups for individuals with clinical eating disorders as well as for those who have some eating disorder symptoms. Although the organization is located in New York at 418 East 76th Street, 10021 (212-734-1114), it has a national focus and has information about treatment and self-help groups nationwide.

Appendix C: Calorie Expenditure Chart

When you use the following chart, you should keep a number of issues in mind. Although weight has more of an impact on calories burned then gender, men will often burn more calories than females because of their greater muscle mass—the differences are slight, however. For example, in the case of downhill skiing, females generally will burn about .6 fewer calories per minute than men. Other activities vary by gender in the same proportions; males, for example, will burn about 1.2 more calories per minute running at a 5.5-minute-mile pace.

Also, exercise equipment that effectively simulates activities such as cycling, running, rowing, and the like will generally burn the same amount of calories as the actual activity. But certain machines, such as the Stairmaster, that keep a constant pace may lead to more caloric expenditure in the same time period.

CALORIE EXPENDITURE CHART

Caloric Expenditure Per Minute for Various Forms of Exercise As Function of Body Weight

Activity	110	125	140	Weight 155	170	185	200
Aerobic dance	8.4	9.4	10.9	11.4	12.9	13.9	15.0
Bicycling (5.5 mph)	3.2	3.6	4.0	4.5	4.9	5.3	5.9
Bicycling (rapid pace)	8.5	9.5	11.0	12.0	13.0	14.0	15.5
Golf	4.3	4.8	5.3	6.0	6.5	7.1	7.4
Karate	9.8	10.9	12.1	13.8	15.0	16.2	17.9
Rowing (strenuous)	5.2	5.8	6.4	7.3	7.9	8.5	9.2
Running (11½-minute mile)	6.8	7.6	8.8	9.6	10.5	11.3	12.5
(8-minute mile)	10.8	11.9	13.1	14.8	16.0	17.1	18.9
(5½-minute mile)	14.5	16.2	17.9	20.5	22.3	24.0	26.6
Skiing (cross-country/including uphill)	13.7	15.3	17.0	19.5	21.1	22.7	24.4
(downhill)	5.3	5.7	6.8	7.5	8.0	8.6	9.6
Squash	10.6	11.9	13.1	15.1	16.3	17.6	18.9
Swimming	7.8	8.7	9.7	11.1	12.0	12.9	13.9
Tennis	5.5	6.4	7.1	7.7	8.4	9.0	9.7
Walking (leisurely)	4.0	4.5	5.2	5.7	6.2	6.6	7.1
(uphill)	6.1	6.8	7.5	8.6	9.3	10.0	10.8

Appendix D: Competitive Training Schedule

Nancy Gengler is the head squash professional at New York Sports Clubs in Manhattan. Nancy has been highly ranked in American squash for the past ten years, and she won the 1989 National Women's Hardball Championship. The following is her training plan for that tournament, which involved playing six matches that ranged in time from 30 to 110 minutes over four days. This schedule gives a realistic picture of how even intense, professional training does not need to cross over the line between optimal and excessive exercise programs.

Nancy began her training for the September 15 tournament on July 1. Her concern from the beginning was to avoid overtraining. To reduce her exercise load at that time, she discontinued giving lessons to players other than beginners. Each week, Nancy completely stopped all exercise on Sundays and made sure that her Saturday trips to the gym took no more than half a day. Three weeks before the tournament, Nancy reduced her training to the point where she wouldn't feel the effects of the workout the next day. She did this to avoid overtraining, staleness, and injury. Five days before the tournament, she stopped all training completely.

During Nancy's training period, she practiced both aerobic workouts and resistance/strength training. *She alternated days for each type of exercise.* Her peak level of training is presented below. (Keep in mind that Nancy started the program already in excellent shape.)

TRAINING SCHEDULE

AEROBIC DAYS

- Twenty minutes of exercise biking. Typically five minutes of warm-up and then alternation of thirty seconds of sprinting followed by fifteen seconds of slow speed recovery time.
- 3.5 miles of running at a moderate pace on a flat dirt track twice per week only.
- At the end of the training period, alternate 400-yard sprints with 400-yard slow jogs (interval training).
- Twenty minutes of jumping rope on nonrunning days only.
- Alternate thirty-second bursts with fifteen-second recovery periods.

Note the consistent burst and recovery approach in Nancy's aerobic program. Nancy refused to exhaust herself with extended periods of anaerobic effort without recovery periods. She knew that exhaustive training does not effectively build a base of conditioning but serves only to deteriorate physical conditioning through fatigue. Also note that aerobic workouts took only forty to forty-five minutes per day—more effort than this would not have a benefit.

RESISTANCE STRENGTH CONDITIONING DAYS

- Upper-body free weights. Three sets of lifts at a weight that induces muscle failure at the end of the set but not before.

- Situps. Sets of fifteen.

Try for twenty sets of fifteen per day on resistance training days.

- Leg lifts. Sets of twenty with a two-and-a-half-pound weight.

Try for ten sets of twenty per day on resistance training days.

Note the consistent approach to Nancy's resistance/ strength conditioning: She worked out only to a level that induced muscle failure and then she stopped. She used multiple sets of fewer repetitions rather than extended periods of trying to lift the same weight.

SQUASH TECHNIQUE PRACTICE (every day)

- Stroke practice. Hit by self for twenty minutes.

- Court sprints. Chase imaginary balls for one minute and then rest for thirty seconds. Ten minutes per day.

MATCH PLAY

- Two hard matches per week scheduled on aerobic training days. If feeling tired after matches, skip aerobic training completely.

Nancy believes that due to the combination of cross-training and the discontinuation of hard training at the right time, she was able to win the tournament without losing one game and without running out of energy during play.

Although when not training for a tournament Nancy may spend as much as eight hours a day on the squash court, there are several indicators that she is not addicted to exercise. During her training period, Nancy was able to reduce her workouts at the right time, with positive effects. If she felt tired after playing a hard match, she skipped the rest of her training. If she felt like taking a day off, she did. When she pulled a muscle playing a match in July, she took three days off; when she got the flu in August, she rested and did not exercise at all. When Nancy was at her peak level of training, she was actually spending less time exercising than when she is simply teaching squash all day. Nonaddicted exercisers like Nancy can periodically adjust their training schedules to fit their health and personal needs; addicted exercisers cannot.

Chapter Notes

CHAPTER 5

1. K. Brownell, J. Rodin, and J. Wilmore, "Eat, Drink, and Be Worried?" *Runner's World* 23 (August 1988): 28–34.

CHAPTER 6

1. Nancy Kilodny, *When Food's a Foe* (Boston: Little, Brown & Co., 1987), p. 49.
2. _____, "A Hidden Epidemic," *Sports Illustrated* 71 (August 14, 1989): 16.
3. Anne Katherine, *Anatomy of a Food Addiction* (New York: Prentice Hall Press, 1991), p. 159.
4. Rebecca Prussin and Philip Harvey, "Depression, Dietary Restraint, and Binge Eating in Female Runners," *Addictive Behaviors* (1991).

CHAPTER 7

1. Prevention Magazine Editors, *Fitness for Everyone* (Emmaus, Penn.: Rodale Press, 1984), p. 52.
2. Beth Livermore, "Is It Chemistry or Body Heat?" *Health* 21 (December 1989): 54.
3. L. F. Tomasi, J. A. Peterson, G. P. Pettit, et al., "Women's Response to Army Training," *The Physician and Sportsmedicine* 5 (1977): 32–37.
4. P. A. Whiteside, "Men's and Women's Injuries in Comparable Sports," *The Physician and Sportsmedicine* 8 (1980): 130.

5. B. Drinkwater, K. Nilson, et al., "Bone Mineral Content of Amenorrheic and Eumenorrheic Athletes," *The New England Journal of Medicine* 311 (August 2, 1984): 277–81.
6. Livermore, ibid., 56.
7. Ibid., 55.
8. Ibid.

CHAPTER 8

1. Beth Livermore, "Give Yourself a Lift," *Health* 21 (December 1989): 56.

Index

213